THE **HUNT** BI

LIFE AFTER THE DEATH OF SELLING

How to Thrive in the New Era of Sales

TOM SEARCY and CARAJANE MOORE

Revised Second Edition

INDIE BOOKS INTERNATIONAL

Printed in the United States of America.

ISBN-10: 1-947480-76-6
ISBN-13: 978-1-947480-76-6

Cover designed by Joni McPherson, mcphersongraphics.com

INDIE BOOKS INTERNATIONAL, INC.
2424 VISTA WAY, SUITE 316
OCEANSIDE, CA 92054
www.indiebooksintl.com

TABLE OF CONTENTS

Author's Note: How to Read This Book 1
Introduction: Is Selling Really Dead? 3

Part 1: Executive Sales Leadership 7

Chapter 1: Defining Leadership in the New World of Sales 9
Chapter 2: Mapping the Strategy for Executive Leadership 18
Chapter 3: Creating Organizational Confidence 28
Chapter 4: Providing Resources 35
Chapter 5: Determining When to Change Course 48
Chapter 6: Leading Transformational Change 52

Part 2: Sales Management 58

Chapter 7: The Three Trends of Sales 60
Chapter 8: Managing the Selling Process 65
Chapter 9: Hiring for the New Sales World 75
Chapter 10: Coaching for Sales Performance 83

Part 3: Sales Maximization 93

Chapter 11: The Role of the Modern Sales Professional 95
Chapter 12: Securing the Executive Sponsor 102
Chapter 13: Assembling a Buyer's Table of High-Level Influencers 110
Chapter 14: Getting Reconnaissance Right 118
Chapter 15: Managing the Process 133
Chapter 16: Facilitating Trust and Solutions 146

Final Thoughts 156
Works Cited 157
Acknowledgements 158

Author's Note: How to Read This Book

To make the reading of this book easier, we have taken a single author's voice.

One of the challenges of writing a book about the sea change in selling is recognizing that this book will have very different readers.

Organization leaders such as CEOs, company presidents, and business owners want a picture of the future at a strategic and market level. Vice presidents and senior sales managers want to know how to manage people, process, and performance through this change and achieve their targets. Salespeople want information on how to be more successful in the very next sales call, proposal, or closing meeting. In essence, we're talking about three different readers concerned with vision, strategy or tactics respectively.

My initial thought was to write three books. After some consideration, however, I realized that there's a lot of blurring of lines in the roles of selling. I also think it's important for all three mindsets to have exposure to one another, as the new world of selling demands a deeply organized and orchestrated approach across strata. And finally, people take on new roles. Someone immersed in tactics today might be challenged to think in terms of strategy or vision tomorrow, and vice versa. I decided to organize the book in three large parts so that by reviewing the Contents and the introductions to each of the book's parts, readers could determine which material they felt was most relevant to their needs and interests.

Here's what I recommend: Read the book's Introduction; then read the Introductions for each of the book's three Parts. Most likely, you will resonate with one Part more than the other two. That's OK—go ahead and read the chapters in that Part first. Then use the book's Contents to guide you to the chapters that focus on topics of interest to you. Don't feel you must read the whole book in order to benefit from it. Selling is in a period of significant change, and those chapters that may not be relevant to you today may be of interest at some point in the future.

Of course, you could also just read it from beginning to end! Whatever you decide to do, my greatest hope is that this book will help you better navigate the changing world of selling and that these notes will help you better navigate my book.

Tom Searcy
Miami, Florida
January 2015

Introduction: Is Selling Really Dead?

We've all heard the phrase "The King is dead, long live the King!" This was originally declared in France when King Charles VI died. The first part of the declaration announced the King's death, while the second part referred to his heir, Charles VII, who immediately succeeded to the throne. The famous words have parallels in our world today: when one thing passes, another replaces it.

And so it is with selling. When one era of selling passes, another immediately begins. I did not write *Life After the Death of Selling* to say that selling, at its core, is dead. I wrote it to explain that the era of selling we have been operating in is dead, and we must equip ourselves with the tools necessary to be successful in sales in the new era that is upon us.

The world of sales didn't change in a vacuum. It changed because the world of buying changed. When I began writing this book, I reflected on the past decade and saw very specific developments occurred that changed how selling was performed overall, how revenue was generated, and how companies incorporated these changes through their sales management. Significant shifts in the B2B buying process have transformed selling as we know it. In this book, I lay out how the world of sales must adapt going forward into the next decade.

In order to move forward, we have to look back just a bit. The original sales process was a barter system. Two people in similar geographies would exchange products or services. Each would get something that he or she did not have or did not specialize in from someone who did. Geographical distance often dictated the cost, based on the effort and expense of getting the product or service from seller to buyer.

As modes of transportation were developed and the ability to travel became more prevalent, people from various cultures commuted long distances to bring goods to their communities that could not be manufactured locally. They might bring raw materials, components, or finished goods. Despite more efficient travel and trade, geography was still the dominant driver of deal terms and the chief factor that separated the buyer and the seller.

This evolution of global trade created the 1.0 sales world: the seller had the greatest knowledge of the competitive products and offerings available within a given region or locale; therefore, the seller set pricing. A salesperson would specialize in one product or service and would give a perfectly scripted presentation to a potential buyer in hope of selling that product or service. The seller's assessment of competitive offerings was rarely challenged by the buyer because the buyer did not have access to relevant information to compare two similar offerings.

Those days are over.

Today, geography is no longer a barrier to sales transactions—or if it is, it is only a limited barrier. Sales transactions are processed through computers, facilitated through rapid delivery, and financed through mechanisms that occur with the swipe of a credit card. The barriers to product information have fallen as well. Global access to information and the technologies that facilitate exchange of information allow buyers to know and assess the differences between one product or service and another in order to make an educated buying decision. They can read case studies and testimonials from previous buyers and compare prices. Geography no longer controls access to raw materials, goods, or information.

In the past, salespeople met face-to-face and developed relationships with buyers. They could communicate their experience and unique knowledge of a product and service directly to a buyer. There was a place for charisma and passion in the sales process. Salespeople were able to look someone in the eye, read the situation, and make small adjustments in framing and facilitating the buyer's decision process. They could apply negotiation tactics for agreeing on price and terms, as well as choose from an array of communication and leverage techniques that they found effective and were part of their personal selling style.

Today, those of us in sales have less opportunity to forge these relationships with buyers. Recent studies indicate that 57 percent of the buyer's decision has already been made before meeting with the salesperson (CEB Global 2015). What does this data mean? It means that buyers who are looking to make a purchase have already gone online, looked at comparative values across a variety of products and platforms, considered the available vendors, read customer reviews about the service, product and company, and have come to some baseline conclusions before meeting with a salesperson. Bottom line: almost 60 percent of what was traditionally considered to be selling has been completed without interaction with a salesperson. This phenomenon is expected to increase as technology continues to be utilized in consumer purchasing, and it is estimated that by 2020, customers will manage 85 percent of their purchasing transactions without talking to a human (Hubspot 2015).

This shift frustrates sales leaders for obvious reasons. Salespeople have many fewer opportunities to meet personally with buyers, develop relationships with them, and facilitate buyers' decisions. Instead, the buying process has been standardized to the point where an Excel spreadsheet winds up replacing the salesperson, laying out features and benefits, prices and vendors—which almost always results in a lowest-price based purchase.

Despite all of these changes, however, the world of selling has not yet transformed the way it operates to respond to this "new normal." There are still territorially organized sales forces that are limited by geography, even when no geographic barrier is necessary. Sales as a profession is not dealing with the public's diminished view of the role of the salesperson as a source of valuable information.

This little history lesson has critical implications. One is the looming death of the territorial sales rep, manufacturer's rep, dealer, and distributor in their current form. This outcome alone is so disruptive and so demoralizing to most organizations that they are paralyzed when it comes to devising a strategy for dealing with this transformational change. Another implication is that transaction processing will be valued more for its efficiency and accuracy and less for the "personal touch" of a sales representative. These changes affect organizations as a whole and must be fully realized and addressed by all levels: organizational leadership, sales management, and the reps themselves.

In the buyer-driven economy, if you want to make big sales, your company must begin solving big problems for high-level executives. I am talking about assembling a team to craft a unique solution, or to help to develop a unique product component or service in order to offer benefit and advantage to the buying company. Doing this takes time, people, strategy, management, and leadership. The world of selling is no longer about communicating, or bidding, or relationships only. Selling is now about strategic engagement. To accomplish that, the sales leader (or even the CEO) will need to adopt new technologies and approaches, and establish a new culture in the company from the top down. Sales managers will need to be able to make decisions in the sales process about which opportunities to hunt, because hunting big opportunities is costly. Sales reps will need to learn a different set of skills for speaking in the language of more senior executives.

The days of selling in the traditional sense of the word are over. We live in a world in which terms have become dangerously commoditized. The world of sales itself has been commoditized to the point where both a restaurant server and a top seller in a large sales organization could both receive a "Salesperson of the Month" award. We need a new framework that redefines what selling is today. The roles and responsibilities of people at each level then need to be redefined in this new framework. My goal is to give you new tools, techniques, approaches, and a roadmap for being more successful in the new sales environment.

Part 1: Executive Sales Leadership

Introduction

At the very beginning of my career, a mentor told me that an owner or CEO had a responsibility to do four things unique to that position:

- Set goals
- Allocate resources
- Provide direction
- Break logjams

Although not perfect advice, it has been very helpful to me throughout my career in providing guidelines for choosing my highest priorities and making the best use of my time.

Looking back over a career that entailed running four very fast-growth companies and aiding the leaders of almost 1000 other fast-growth companies, I want to add one more to that short list:

- Drive revenue strategy

I have been surprised at the number of company leaders who believe that revenue does not deserve its own category—that it in fact is a subset of the other four. For growing companies, *revenue is the prime mover*. It creates the opportunity, capacity, and resources for all other functions to have oxygen and purpose. To some of you who are reading this book, that is a long-understood truth. For others, it may be a truth that is inconvenient at best. But I'm here to tell you: in this new world of selling, leadership means getting your hands dirty, down in the guts of the revenue-generating machine.

I wrote this part of the book to give you a roadmap for your changing role. Specifically, I aim to answer a few key questions:

1. What is your job as a leader of change in your company, and how is that different from the job you are currently doing?

2. What decisions are uniquely yours to make that you may have delegated or shared with your leadership team in the past?
3. How can you change the growth capacity of your company and its leaders?
4. What are the most important indicators to watch during this change, and what do they mean?

Finally, you will note that I used the word "driving" not "setting" revenue strategy. Your role is not to lead from the back or from 30,000 feet in this changing revenue environment. Your job is to be at the front, leading change from the ground. The chapters that follow are intended to help you define how you will lead for change.

Chapter 1: Defining Leadership in the New World of Sales

What is leadership? Much has been written about it, but when I look for definitions, I find all sorts of wonderful ideas, phrases, and pithy comments, but not a lot of meat. I appreciate these succinct, meaningful quotations that I can post around my office and share with others, but in the fast-paced, results-oriented world we live in today, I also want an action plan: a clear picture of what I need to do. In this chapter, we're going to talk about leadership in the world of sales. Some of the concepts will be familiar to you, but I hope that we can challenge just a few of those that you have accepted in the past so that you can see why your role as sales leader continues to be critical, but in some new ways.

In the past, the effective executive leader had a clear vision, efficiently carved out territories, laid out a compensation plan, and made certain that marketing was providing the tools and resources the salespeople needed. Those days are fading. One thing that hasn't changed for leadership is that you must define what is possible and then inspire people to achieve it. In today's buyer's economy, your role as sales leader is more strategic and critical than it has been in the past. Let's talk about some of the ways this plays out.

The Chinese Lion Leader

If you walked into my office today, you would see a large papier-mâché Chinese lion head hanging from the ceiling. You've probably seen something like it in a parade or on television. Typically, a Chinese lion costume consists of a very, very large mask worn by the person in the front, with five, seven, nine, or eleven dancers lined up behind the leader under a long length of decorated fabric. The dance consists of this line of people moving in an undulating, "push me, pull you" kind of way. The line of dancers elongates and shortens like an accordion as the dancers move through the crowd, sometimes bumping into each other, sometimes going in different directions, as the lion accordion-dances on its way.

I use the Chinese lion dance to describe to sales leaders what it is like to be a part of a growing organization. The question is, why is the dance the way that it is? Why are the dancers bumping into each other, moving apart and together? Why do some go left and some right? The reason is simple: *only the person at the very front of the lion costume can see out through the eyes and knows the path ahead.* Everyone else is under the fabric with their hands on the shoulders of the person in front of them, hoping to figure out what steps they should take next by looking at their neighbor's feet.

As a sales leader, you need to recognize that this is how your organization operates. Only you can see the future, and you're communicating this information to your organization in an extremely noisy environment known as the marketplace. With all sorts of cacophony going on around you, your job is to communicate whether your team should go left or right, move faster or slower, keep going or stop. It's not easy, but it's absolutely necessary. Without your ability to see the future and then communicate where to go next, you will not be able to advance effectively, and certainly not attain a pace that beats your competitors.

Sales leaders must paint the picture of the future. Where are we going, who are the customers we will serve, how will we serve them, and what will their unique needs be? Providing answers to these questions will keep your organization moving along on the right path, and allow you to win in this new world of sales.

Painting the Picture of the Future

This idea of defining what is possible and then inspiring people to achieve it makes a lot of sense, but it is important for you as the sales leader to create clarity. Your executive peers are asking:

- What will our customers be like?
- What will the future of our business be like?
- What will our sales team and sales process look like in the future?

These questions are about making structural responses to a changing environment. To motivate and mobilize for structural change, you must start with the prime mover of change: the customer. *Painting the picture of the future starts with picturing your customer in the future.*

In the past, when trying to forecast the sales climate, we looked at our markets, our products, our services, and our cycle for delivering our goods to the marketplace over time. Often, we would widen our scope to include the activities of our competitors: what they were doing; where they were going; how they were sourcing; what they were developing. Our efforts would expand and contract depending on whether we were the market leader, the market follower, or at the bottom of the market trying to get a foothold.

Today, your job as the executive leader is to be the fortuneteller for your business. You must figure out what the customer will need not today, but tomorrow and the day after that. Then you must build your messaging, your solutions, and the picture of your company's sales identity around what your customer will need in the future. Your customer's future needs determine whom you will serve, what you will provide, and what mechanism you will use to provide it. In the past, these decisions were often made by engineering, operations, or maybe marketing. Now, executive leaders working with sales leaders to make these decisions because the sales leaders are in contact with customers and prospects, and therefore in a position to understand most clearly customers' needs.

Now, I may make some enemies around this next statement, but I don't care:

Choosing the destination for the future of the organization is not a collaborative process.

I don't think Christopher Columbus boarded his boats and asked all of his sailors, "Where do you want to go?" Instead, he boarded the boats and said something like, "We're going to the New World. It's going to be fantastic when we get there. Hoist the sails, put in the oars, grab hold of the keel, and let's go."

That is your responsibility. So, what is the new world of selling as it relates to your business? As the leader, you're going to seek counsel about that, but you will be the one to make the final decision about what's happening out there and where your team is headed. Of course, your specialists will help you to figure out the options and the plans for how you're going to do it. You'll need engineering. You'll need marketing. You'll need operations, and you'll need all of the other parts of your organization to help you to figure out the "how" your company can deliver the future. But selection of the destination is up to you.

Building a Framework for Making Decisions

In the new world of selling and on this great journey I'm describing, a series of choices, or decisions, will have to be made. They include:

- The companies you want to work with
- The solutions you want to offer
- The financial rewards you will seek

Some issues are not on the table; for example: the mission of the organization, the vision for the company, and your company's values. These should have been decided a long time ago as a part of the overall development of the organization's culture and value system.

Designing your framework for making these decisions is your responsibility. One way to think of decisions is as a series of tradeoffs that you make as a company; for example, choosing what business are you in versus what business are you not in. Of course, decisions can't be made in a vacuum. You'll want to assess how market changes and offerings and competitors affect your choice. By setting up a framework for how you will make choices and decisions before you actually have to make them, you are charting a course rather than just reacting to a storm.

The opposite of setting up a framework in advance is what I refer to as "circumstantial opportunism." That means that you just take things as they come, making decisions on a one-off basis from the perspective of the current moment alone. If you're lucky, it might work at times. But I don't recommend steering your ship that way on an ongoing basis.

A framework for choices, designed by you as the organization's leader, allows for consistency and integrity across the entire sales organization, including those who are tangentially supportive of the sales efforts. Everyone will be rowing in the same direction, optimizing your chances of reaching your destination.

Some of the most important choices you will make and live with are more gut than science. I hate that. I like the idea that there is precision and process for arriving at conclusions. In some areas of leadership, however, the choices are less clear and more personal. Three areas of leadership that are softer include talent, culture and the stretch.

1. Talent

Why would I put talent in the area of leadership? Because I think that the business function of talent selection, management, sourcing, and development has been neglected in the last few years. In contrast, enormous amounts of time and money have been spent on formulating things like job descriptions, organizational charts, interview protocols, and testing. I find that these investments have a tendency to set hiring and performance standards of "good enough." Good enough is not necessarily the standard you're looking for. Business leadership must hold a standard to define "great." Let your competitors stick with good enough. You will be hiring a cut above by focusing on intangibles.

You are looking for a team of specialists operating under a system that allows for interchangeability among the trained team members. Now, I know that the Navy SEAL Team 6 metaphor has been used to the point of exhaustion, even though it is a very valuable metaphor. But it's a useful concept to keep in mind that if you were going out into the marketplace to sell your larger accounts and launch opportunities with the team, you would want to take a team of the best of your best – the most specialized to their function – in order to be successful.

Executive sales leaders have the final say in decision-making. Leaving this to someone else, such as human resources or a field manager, is to put your entire success as sales executive at risk. In the race for the biggest opportunities, we will not lose or win against a competitor by a mile; we'll win or lose by inches. The inches by which you win or lose will be dictated by the quality of the people you have on your team.

"Good enough" will get you to that disappointing space known as second place. I refer to this as the crash site of failure. If you want to be first, then you will take personal responsibility in your leadership role for the selection and the final word on talent.

2. Culture

What does culture mean? I believe that the culture of an organization is reflected in what is rewarded, what is penalized, what is elevated, and what is made fun of. For example, whether you fire a customer who needs to be fired or keep a customer who should be fired, both of these are culture-defining moments. How you react tells your organization what you'll put up with and what you won't, what risks you're willing to take and what risks you'll shy away from.

Most of the time, an organization's culture is easily observable in the behaviors of its people. To survive in the new market, you are going to have to shift the culture of your organization. One of the hard parts about that is that a culture is often based on a shared history of what works. That means that, for good or for bad, your people are able to look at what has worked in the past and base their decisions upon that: here's what works to get me promoted, to make my bonus, to win a deal with a customer, to get a discount on price so that I can keep a current customer happy, and so on. Culture permeates small things and large things across the spectrum of decisions that are made in an organization, especially those that are repeatedly made. Those day-to-day decisions form the context in which the organization sits, and we call that context culture.

You are trying to take your organization into a new culture, which means that you have to get your team to do something different than what has been done in the past. As I write this, I am picturing two dinosaurs observing the first flakes of snow. One dinosaur looks at the other one and says, "Does it seem like it's getting cold to you?" And the other dinosaur says, "Nah, nah. It's okay. I think it's going to pass." Extinction is what happens when the shared history of what used to work takes us past the point where we need to adapt. If you do not adapt, you will become extinct like the dinosaurs. *Your role in sales leadership is to recognize that the snowflakes are already falling.*

The world is no longer as it was. If you continue to try to sell by hard work, charisma, personal contacts, and your database of people you've done business with in the past, you are going to go extinct. Your ability to be an effective sales leader is, in part, dictated by your ability to increase the capacity of your organization to change.

An organization's capacity for change shapes its speed of growth. Only you can lay out a plan of what the future will look like. Then you need to ask the question, "What culture do we need to have in order to win in that future?" Defining the culture that you need to have will cause you to address all of the other issues I raised above when defining culture: what do we reward, what do we punish, what do we elevate, what do we diminish, what do we support, and what do we turn away from?

As part of creating that new world of culture, you will need to capture and memorialize the stories of success as they happen. These need to be the relevant folklore in the six-month and twelve-month windows going forward. Do not simply rely on success stories from the company's long-ago history or of the last ten years. That history is of diminishing value as we all prepare ourselves for a rapidly shifting future.

3. The Stretch

We've talked about a lot of things in this chapter, but I want to return to one of its core principles—the idea of painting the picture of the future—and close with the reminder that it is your responsibility as a leader to define *what is possible*. And that may stretch your people further than they thought they could go.

Every good coach knows that if you let athletes pick their moment to give their best effort, they will fall short of their potential. Again and again, high school coaches talk about how when athletes have been pushed hard, whether in training, in a game, or at a meet, they put out their best effort ever. When that happens, they often come to their coach afterwards and say, "I didn't think I could do it." And the coach says, "I knew you could."

One of your key responsibilities as sales leader is to define for the people in your organization what is possible. It's a lonely role, with lots of resisters. People will say, "We can't make that many changes that quickly," "We can't do the kinds of things that you're talking about," "We'll never be able to get the market to respond," and so on. But, as you know, if you're going to get change to happen for your organization, you have to define what is possible by declaring what you and the organization are going to do next and not listen to the resisters who tell you what cannot be achieved. Otherwise, you're just sitting there at the high school track meet, agreeing when someone says that he or she can't run a second faster or can't jump an inch farther.

Yielding, compromising, reasonable coaches do not create world champions. It is the unyielding, the unreasonable, and uncompromising coach who helps push athletes to championship levels of performance.

It is your job to not yield in the face of your team telling you that less is the best they can do. However, it is important to remember that without a realistic plan for achieving it, a stretch goal is simply a waste of time. No one expects an athlete to set records without a rigorous training program. If your goal isn't attached to a clear plan, it is not realistic, and it is not really a goal at all. It is just a number that is bigger than what you have a viable plan to achieve. If you cannot provide justification for how you will attain the goal via a detailed plan with clear assumptions, then you will lose the confidence of your people and will not be able to reach those high levels of achievement. "The stretch" is the difference between what people *think* is possible and what you as their sales leader *know* is possible, and it will be what will help you to succeed.

In conclusion, proximity is the word that best summarizes the role of leadership in the new selling world. Leadership will need to be closer to the market, the customers, and the action. The company will look to leadership to discern what is real change versus what is merely an "idea du jour." Make no mistake, as you declare where your organization is going, what is rewarded or punished, and how your company will respond to the shifting currents, everyone in your organization will be watching. Leadership from the front will be noticed and followed.

Chapter 2: Mapping the Strategy for Executive Leadership

There's an old saying that "culture eats strategy for breakfast." I think that's a poor tradeoff. I also don't believe that it's an either/or proposition. Successful organizations have both culture and strategy. In fact, strategy is a part of the culture.

Strategy is defined as a plan of action or a policy designed to achieve a major or overall aim. While that general definition offers some sense of direction for sales, a sales leadership strategy is more about defining one's advantage: what advantage do we have, based on what our organization offers, the needs of our customers, the weaknesses of our competitors, the changes that are happening in technology, regulation, or other circumstances, that we can then leverage to get an advantage?

In addition, you as the executive leader must constantly redefine and seek advantage in an increasingly fast-paced climate of change. This means that you need to develop a culture within your organization that can shift strategy with a speed that mirrors the pace of change in your marketplace, with the dual goals of generating new customers and growing your business with current customers. As I mentioned in the Introduction, this means determining how to solve "big problems for high-level executives."

The idea of selling all things to all people is a holdover from the old world of selling, or the world of the open marketplace. Every village had a marketplace where manufacturers, farmers, and other purveyors of goods and services would come to barter and exchange. In that marketplace, you could sell anything to anybody who had a coin. That's no longer a viable methodology, especially in the bigger opportunities. The digital marketplace, which never closes and is ever expanding, allows you the chance to hang out your digital shingle and operate your store 24/7 all over the virtual world. But just being open for business—even in the market that never stops growing and never sleeps—is not selling.

These days, pretty much anyone can open an Internet storefront, put an offering out in the marketplace, and set up a mechanism for transacting business. That's no longer what we call selling. We're also not talking about the marketplace of the structured purchase, in which you undertake a process to qualify as a certified vendor to an organization that then allows you the opportunity of participating in buying processes such as RFPs, procurement, purchasing and other mechanisms of structured process. No, what we're talking about here is a much higher level of sales.

The higher-level sale requires a greater level of efficiency than the hang-out-your-shingle, sell-all-things-to-all-people approach. Why? Because you're using more resources to hunt opportunity in the marketplace. You may need a larger team, it may take more time and cycles to meet with all the people on your clients' teams, and you'll need time and resources to gather more insight and information to shape your offering to a given prospect. That all adds up to more investment per sale. For that reason, you must be as efficient as possible in your prospecting and in your selling process. Your first step is to figure out whom you will target as your potential customer, and more importantly, whom you will avoid.

If you let your salespeople run amok in the marketplace, calling on whomever they choose, you will get a lower yield because there is little selectivity and no focus on efficiency. However, if you tighten up your overall filter for assessing the marketplace and ensure that the prospect opportunities are highly qualified, you will have greater control over the selling process, the yield, and the overall effectiveness of your salespeople.

Let's agree upon a fundamental truth. There is a built-in frictional cost to the acquisition and onboarding of every new customer, but the higher-level sale offers a greater margin available over which to amortize that expense. The new market recognizes that there's a separation between transaction facilitation, process compliance, and selling. For you, this translates into segmentation of your target by business channel.

The organization leader in today's sales world looks at every sales rep, every sales function and system, and every marketing effort in the marketplace not as an expense, but rather as an investment, similar to the way that investment bankers look at a portfolio. They regularly assess each investment, asking, "What is the efficiency of my return on this investment?" They then use this information to invest more heavily in things that return a higher rate, and eliminate those that return a lower rate.

In the past, our investment in the selling process was mostly limited to the selection and hiring of salespeople. We would evaluate their sales track records, keep those we considered "winners," and let go those who were "losers." But in today's complex sales environment in which you're solving all kinds of problems for much bigger buyers, you have to evaluate not just the salespeople, but the selling process, any supporting technologies, and all of the subject matter experts who participate in the overall process to land that much larger account. You will have to make a much deeper level of investment in the selling process before you can assess whether or not you're getting the returns you were hoping to get from investing in that particular account.

In this chapter, we'll explore five questions that you need to answer regularly, and with an increasing volume of data, in order to evaluate the effectiveness of your strategy. When you succeed in answering these questions to their fullest, you will be in a position to step ahead of your competitors and secure an advantage in the marketplace.

1. Which customers should we be targeting?

There was a time when the answer to this question was defined loosely. Geography, industry segment, and revenue size were enough to create a target list of prospects for a sales representative to call upon. It pretty much came down to: "Do they buy what we have, and can they pay for it?"

In the buyer-driven economy, buyers are less curious about sourcing providers of products or solutions that they believe they fully understand the specifications for. Often they have commoditized their needs and delegated the process to purchasing for facilitation. In order to get a senior decision maker's attention and support, we need to understand the target prospect's deeper market problems and be able to show that expertise.

Too often the approach to selecting prospects or targets has been one of "could, should, and would": the prospect company "could" buy what we have because it has purchased this product or service in the past or is doing so now, we are confident that the prospect company "should" buy from us because we are better than our competitors in some way, and the prospect company "would" buy from us if we could overcome some obstacle(s). This approach focuses on us. That is a bad starting place in the new world of selling.

Meaningful targeting focuses less on your economic drivers and more upon your relevance to the problem the prospect executive needs to have solved. If you can solve the prospect's problem, the buying process always moves faster. When you focus on the problem as the defining criteria, you are more successful. Accordingly, here are some better targeting questions than geography, industry, and budget:

- **Does the prospect know that the organization has a problem?** The "old" model of selling was often one of comparative presentation: the seller shows a solution described as being better than what competitors offer, and then asks the buyer to compare and choose the better option. This only works if the buyer believes there is a problem. Few executives in companies are taking meetings to compare ideas in areas in which they do not see a problem. A salesperson may get a meeting through a referral or because your companies are currently doing business in a different area, but true support for the selling process will not occur if the prospect does not know from the very first meeting that there is a problem.

- **Does the prospect have a problem that we solve?** Sales people are sometimes best at selling solutions that we do not have or that we would have to customize heavily in order to provide. As an executive, this can be vexing. When sales people are allowed to pick their targets by criteria other than problem, they will sell to anyone with a problem regardless of whether your company solves that problem. This clogs up the system with poorly qualified opportunities that waste the time and patience of the organization.

- **Is the problem significant enough that the prospect may be willing to undergo the pain of change?** The research comparing executives of different generations shows irrefutably that executives now are being asked to cover more ground in business than in the past. More personnel, markets and areas of responsibility mean that those executives are only interested in the hottest fires. They may be interested in what you have to say, but there will be delays in additional meetings and consideration in the selling process unless the problem that you solve is one of their fires that is burning most brightly.

- **Does the prospect need the problem solved within the next six to twelve months?** The greater the need for a speedy solution, the brighter burns the prospect of a sale. If there is not a need for a change within the next six to twelve months, that is a good indicator that you should move on. In today's business climate, generally speaking, in that period of time there will be big changes in who is buying, what problem is being solved, and what the prospect's competitive landscape looks like. You can spin your wheels contacting and visiting those prospects who do not need a solution in six months to a year, or you can focus the time on something else.

Defining your target selection criteria by your answers to these questions will have three key benefits for your company. Your company will be more efficient in the selling process. Your salespeople will have a clear definition of and focus on what a successful first meeting looks like—namely, getting the answer to those four questions. Finally, by eliminating slow "no's" and "maybes," all of you will have more time and resources to assign to high-potential opportunities.

2. What is our message?

If you want to know what your message *shouldn't* be in the world of large account selling and solving big problems for big customers, just visit your website. Your website is, in essence, a twenty-first century version of the farmer's booth at the medieval village market. You are telling everyone in the market that you, for example, sell corn. And guess what? If I visit the online booths of four other corn sellers, I will find that they're all hawking the same quality of corn, at the same volume, in the same marketplace. Don't believe me? Ask a website design firm to help you figure out what kind of website you should have. One of the first things they will ask for is a list of your five to ten biggest competitors. What are they doing with that information? They're going to look at all of your competitors' websites. What language and examples are used? What products, services, and solutions are offered? They'll take the best ideas they can find and compare what you're going to bring to the marketplace to what has already been brought to the marketplace by your competitors.

We all recognize this as commoditization: everyone is out in the marketplace sounding alike, solving the same problems in the same way. Since 78 percent of B2B buyers go directly to vendors' websites (Oracle Marketing Cloud 2015; ChatterJee and Gaffney 2012), it is extremely important that you figure out how not to sound like everybody else in the marketplace. That's why the responsibility of defining and designing your message is on your shoulders as the sales leader. Managers can figure out what you're selling. Salespeople can figure out the language of your customers. But only you can figure out what you stand for as a selling company, and that it is consistent in all of your marketplace messaging.

One way to do this is to refocus on the fundamental premise that when you are designing solutions for big people who have big problems, you must concentrate on the problems of time, money, and risk. Why? Because time, money, and risk are what senior executives and decision makers in larger firms are paid to solve as priorities of their job. Addressing your clients' priorities will always keep you close to their changing needs. Your messaging comes from that: it states who you are as an organization in terms of the big problems you solve in the marketplace.

Recently one of my clients was shifting from providing construction management services to being relevant and valuable on a market segment by market segment basis. What does that mean? It means the company dramatically shifted all of its messaging away from focusing on the quality of its certification, its longevity, its economic stability, and the aggregate number of years that its senior leaders had been at the firm, and moved instead toward a strong statement about the problems it could solve in each market segment. Why the shift? Because the company's old message sounded like everyone else's.

It is interesting how often our marketplace message focuses on who we are rather than on the problems we can solve for our buyers. That puts the responsibility on the back of our buyers to connect the dots and determine whether who we are matches the problems they have.

Of course, you can't solve your customers' problems without knowing what they are. As the company's sales leader, you are expected to understand your core market's biggest problems regarding competitors, regulations, technology, and market influences. So when you're designing your message, you are speaking not only as an authority on your product or service, but also as an authority on the customer's marketplace and particular concerns.

Marketplace reconnaissance entails your ability to find out data in nearly real time and use it to design a sales strategy reflective of the implications of what is happening in the marketplace. It used to be that reconnaissance was about asking, "What are my competitors doing?" and "What's happening with product pricing?" Now, if you're going to solve big problems for big people, reconnaissance entails understanding what is going on in your customers' industry as well, if not better, than they do. The organizations that offer the biggest, best solutions have more information about what the buyers' real problems are than the buyers themselves do.

3. What is the best resource allocation for growth?

This is a key role of leadership. You must determine what is possible with your company's unique resources, talent, approach, market, and technology, and then push the organization to a stage beyond what your team thinks is possible, into a new reality that *you've* defined as being possible. Remember what I said in Chapter 1 about how a good coach knows what an athlete is capable of doing, sometimes better than the athlete himself or herself?

As you're defining the new reality that stretches your organization's capabilities, you need to be monitoring the risk portfolio that your organization incurs in stretching toward that goal.

Some questions you may ask include:

- How much of our time and energy do we want to put into serving our current customers well and trying to do brand extensions or service and product extensions within that customer base?

- How much of our time and energy do we want to spend participating in structured purchasing processes such as quotes, bids, RFPs, et cetera?

- How much of our time and energy do we want to spend looking for new, big opportunities by hunting down buyers in the marketplace who have big problems?

The answers to these questions have an enormous impact on the structure and resource allocation you design for your company.

In my work with numerous companies, I find that an analysis of market share, customer penetration, and upside opportunity frequently leads to the conclusion that those companies could more than triple in size through more penetration of their current customers. However, their allocation of resources had placed their best solution designers and salespeople in new customer acquisition rather than in customer expansion and penetration. In fact, rarely have I spent time with a CEO or with a company president who thought that the company had sufficient penetration into current customers—yet in case after case, the allocation of resources showed a large disconnect between this understanding and appropriate action.

Similarly, companies that use distributors, dealers, and manufacturer representative organizations for their new customer acquisition efforts are often frustrated in their growth because they do not see new sales; but rather service and recurring purchase revenues. Yet despite knowing the ineffectiveness of their channel partners, they allocate much of their revenues to service rather than selling new customers.

Your role is to look at the facts and change the actions of your organization accordingly. Facts are our friends, even when they are not friendly.

4. How will we measure progress before success?

A sale is a lagging indicator. It is an event that is the result of milestones of progress attained along the way. When you've made a change in your selling approach, once the system is up and operating, then sales demonstrate the system's success. But what about the sometimes long and complex path your organization must follow in advance of the sale? How do you keep everyone moving using a methodology that they have not yet seen work? In Chapter 8, I discuss the key success indicators represented in a dashboard that provides clear milestones in the selling process, showing movement rather than motion, and that can be understood by the entire organization. The most successful users of this system have embraced the idea that a growth culture is one that understands the selling process.

5. How to get the new system working faster?

Three options include:

- **Force the change by eliminating the old system.** Ease the transition, but don't delay it.

- **Compare the new option to scarier options.** People need a framework in which to evaluate the new plan. Show the alternative option as being even scarier than the one you advocate.

- **Show how the implementation of the new plan will be similar to previous successful strategy implementations in the company.**

Employing these tactics ensures that results are achieved, and it's where project leadership and communication have the greatest impact. The positive experience for your organization occurs when people feel that the new plan has been carefully thought out, that its implementation is well controlled, that the process is familiar in its similarity to other successful implementations, and that success is celebrated when milestones are reached, not just at the end result.

You cannot develop a strategy and draw up a roadmap of milestones on the way to your destination if you are disengaged from the data developed from events on the ground that provide you with the information you need to do so. It is your responsibility to get closer to the current in order to have a better view of the flow of events and thus a clearer idea of the future.

That's why I strongly believe that strategy is a hands-on responsibility. Think of it this way: Anyone can steer a boat in calm waters. But in a storm, it takes an experienced hand to make certain that the boat stays upright, that it keeps on course, and that all on board are safe. The new market is forever in a storm. For that reason, your hands must on the wheel. Your voice must heard over the wind. The people who follow you must understand what your commands mean. And you must keep your eyes on the horizon to understand what the next shifting set of circumstances may bring.

Now, here's the thing. If you do this work with a large group of people in your organization, the result will be at best an incrementally different version of what your organization is doing now. The people in your organization will follow a strategy, but they probably cannot define one. Why? Because no matter how talented and willing they are, they are like the Chinese lion I mentioned earlier: moving in a long line behind you. The longer the lion, the harder it is to make the lion dance with the agility needed to make a big change in direction. Charting a strategic vision usually means working with a smaller group of people to define clear answers to the questions I've posed above and map out a plan. That's how your Chinese lion stands the best chance of getting where you need it to go.

Chapter 3: Creating Organizational Confidence

As a professional speaker, I find it amusing to think of motivational speaking as it is commonly conceived and marketed: promising a turnaround in listeners' lives based on the lessons of an inspiring story or a five-step process told in an hour or two.

Don't get me wrong, I believe in inspiration, and I read and appreciate many stories of personal inspiration, perseverance, and achievement. However, when I think about creating confidence in my organization—and over the past thirty years I've run organizations that have achieved dramatic results—I've found that creating confidence comes exclusively from members of the organization achieving together something beyond what they thought they could do.

Let me put it another way. If you want your organization to have confidence, don't just pat them on the back or feed them feel-good messages. Lead them to success. Combining seller training with coaching yields four times the return of training alone. Without on-the-job reinforcement, sellers lose 87 percent of training improvements within one month (Cash 2014).

Do we need to pat people on the back and encourage them? Of course we do. Do we need to show them that we believe in them and that we know that they can accomplish great things? Again, another resounding 'of course.' But if you want to establish organizational confidence around the idea of landing sales and growing your business, nothing will provide greater sustainability than a methodology: a structured process that allows you and your team to win in a predictable fashion again and again.

Over the course of my career, I've had the opportunity to help more than 700 companies land more than $7.5 billion in business. In almost every case, the company was coming from a position of being smaller than its competitors. What gave each company the confidence to succeed was a shared history of having achieved a prior difficult victory. When David beats Goliath, everybody on David's team stands a little taller, has a little more swagger, and talks with more confidence. There's just no substitute for winning.

In the world of sales leadership, your responsibility is to build a structure and a process that creates the opportunity to win. Let's talk about the components that make that happen.

Setting the Higher Bar

If you've ever attended any sort of fight event or watched it on TV—be it boxing, wrestling, judo, or whatever— you've probably heard some loudmouth scream from the rafter seats, "Kill him!" It's pretty distasteful. And it always seems as if it's the person farthest from the ring who has the loudest voice about what the person in the ring should do. If you are going to be a leader in the sales world, then you need to be close to the action and lead from the front on the biggest opportunities that your organization hunts. You must do this for five important reasons:

1. You have the data (and if you don't, you'd better get it). You need data to make the large and small strategic decisions that put your organization in the best position to win. No one else on your team has as much data, experience, and background as you do about what needs to be done.

In bigger opportunities, it's not always clear what to do, and members of your team may not have much experience in knowing what needs to be done at that level of opportunity. You, on the other hand, have past experience and references that give you the insights necessary to make a good decision and to move your organization forward.

2. You display confidence in yourself and in your team by being at the front of the hunt. By being involved in the larger deals that are out there, you set a higher bar for everybody on your team. Sure, it might mean losing. But if you stay in the back, the people in the front will not believe that you are committed to the course you've charted, confident in their ability to execute the plan, and here for the long haul—today and after this deal is done. By being at the front of the hunt, you have told the entire organization that this effort is important, that the team will muster the resources necessary, and that you believe your company is going to win. It's a huge boost of confidence to the rest of the organization when you put your own skin out there in front.

3. You set the pace. When you are landing the biggest opportunities, you are not only setting an example for your organization about what is possible, but you are also setting the pace that is necessary to win. Don't expect your Chinese lion to dance without a head.

Often a CEO continues churning out ideas rather than taking action because his or her thoughts are still evolving based on the input coming from the team. But in order to turn ideas into action, a decision to launch must be made. Give your plan a release date and move forward. You can always decide to add ideas and switch up the strategy later if necessary.

4. You allocate your resources. I find that when sales leaders have their own skin in the game, they marshal many more resources to make certain that their team will win. Many salespeople I have spoken with over the years confide that their biggest obstacle to winning large deals comes not from their competitors or from their prospects, but from the internal inertia of their organization to make the necessary changes and adjustments to win the deal. By putting yourself out in front, you put yourself in a position to marshal the best resources your organization has at its disposal to help ensure that you have success.

5. You learn more. By being out in front, you learn from mistakes and successes alike what it will take to win more big deals. There is no filter to obscure the experience—no retelling of the story to make people look better, no fudging of the facts or falsifying of the records. You were there, you know what happened, and the lessons you and the organization learn can change your process and system going forward.

Provide a Process

In Chapter 1, I rather facetiously scripted the pep talk Christopher Columbus might have given his crew to spur them to set off with him for faraway lands. But I often think about what it really must have been like to be a crew member for the original explorers. At the time, there was no complete understanding of where they were headed, no certain destination, only enough supplies to keep the crew alive a little longer than the duration of the furthest trip away from shore ever taken, and no reliable way to measure progress toward this nebulous goal. If you want to create confidence in your crew, one of the best ways to do that is to provide an articulated process for measuring progress.

An articulated process lets you chart progress even during those periods when your destination isn't in close sight. With an articulated process, you don't just tell your crew that this voyage is going to take seven weeks. You set milestones to reach week by week and explain how to know when those milestones have been reached. You might say that at the end of week one, we'll be able to see these constellations in these particular locations. At the end of week two, we will probably see a change in the color of the water. And so on. When they have an articulated process for achieving what seems to be the impossible, people have the confidence to stay with the process because they see progress against milestones defined by you. Setting the course is the role of senior sales leadership. You are providing that clear, articulated process that gives people confidence to stay on the boat.

Collect the Lessons

When we're sailing unfamiliar waters, we don't always know what we'll encounter along the way. We make the best map we can, follow it with care, and figure out as we go whether we are getting where we need to go. Are we reaching our milestones? If not, why not? Do we need to correct course? We must retain those lessons so that the next time we come this way, we know what to do. Refer to this as the lesson process. It entails simply asking the question, "What have we learned at this point?" Lessons show the progress you have made toward success, but they are also a useful catalog of failed attempts. The combination of what steps have resulted in progress and what have not gives us a refining system.

By building the lesson process into the sales process, we can build a better roadmap with clearer understanding of terrain along the way so that we are an ever-improving organization. I find that in general there is little process analysis of sales that have been won or lost, and too often sales narratives become more like the fishing yarns that are told around the campfire.

When we tell tall tales about sales, we don't capture data or insights that could help us change the process and become more successful. Everything looks like an amazing intersection of luck, timing, and of course our considerable personal skill. Such stories don't build the confidence of an organization because these successes do not feel replicable. If you want to build your team's confidence, you must be with your team, gather the lessons, and apply them to the process so that your team see and believes that it is getting better.

Build a Ladder of Achievement

Executives sometimes tell me that they view their leadership role as "playing devil's advocate." From what I can tell, the devil doesn't need a lot of advocacy. He is perfectly capable of getting to hell on his own. What most organizations need is not a devil's advocate, but an achievement advocate to set them up for success, step by step.

Your job is to figure out how to put the odds in your organization's favor to win the hunt—to land new business and grow your current accounts. One way to do this is to establish opportunities for early wins so that you can increase your team's confidence and encourage those who are willing to learn but reluctant at first to enter the fray.

In *Rocky II*, Rocky's trainer sets up a series of fights for Rocky along the way to the championship fight. The idea was to keep Rocky motivated to train, think, and act like a champion by giving him opportunities to win along the way.

Our version of the Rocky roadmap is saying, "What is the first opportunity where we can apply our processes and systems and win?" Once your team wins that fight, then you ask, "What is the next opportunity? And so on. By building a ladder of achievement, your leadership will build increasing levels of confidence within the organization, investors, stakeholders, and yourself.

Set Up Structure That Adds Value

When I watch organizations reorganize, I'm sometimes reminded of watching my five-year-old sitting at the table and cutting up her least favorite foods into smaller and smaller pieces. She doesn't want to eat the peas or the green beans or the carrots, so she cuts them into little pieces and moves them around on the plate, making it appear that she's done something productive when in fact she hasn't. Businesses do this when they try to make effective changes simply by reshuffling the players or restructuring the organization chart.

If you're going to spend your time and energy creating confidence, any structural adjustments you make need to add clear and specific value. Just keeping everyone busy (i.e., moving them around the plate) is not productive in itself. Think productivity, not merely activity.

In order to engrain confidence into your company's culture, you must consistently be doing these three things:

1. Declare. Brainstorming can be a great creative exercise, but if you have made a decision, you must declare it. Your team needs to know the difference between thinking aloud and declaring the mission to be executed.

2. Decide. Give your idea its initial specifications and release date and move forward. You can always add more ideas later.

3. Delegate. Assign an implementation person or team to execute your vision; then get out of the way.

Plan and Lead, Step By Step

Creating confidence within your organization requires you to take your organization from one level of performance, marketplace awareness, and understanding of what is necessary to win to a very different and higher level.

In order to do that:

- Each step must feel like it's an achievement.
- Each step must be led by you personally.
- Each step must contain applicable lessons that allow the team to perform better in the future.
- Each step must follow a process.
- Any structural change that you make must support your overall mission to take the team from where it is to where it needs to be.

A final note: the ultimate boost in sales confidence comes from involving the entire company in the ownership and growth of the selling process. This means shifting from the idea of, "we will be successful if the Sales Department is successful" to the belief that "we are an organization that succeeds at selling." When the entire company feels that it participates in the selling process, then the entire organization's belief in what is possible for its future changes. Read on to learn how to make that happen.

Chapter 4: Providing Resources

One of the core responsibilities of sales leaders is resource allocation. Now, to understand resource allocation from a position of executive leadership, I want you to think about the idea of hedging and making bets on a Vegas roulette table.

In roulette, a ball is dropped on a spinning wheel marked with numbers and sections colored black or red. Players bet money in the form of chips on where they think the ball will fall: on odd or even numbers, on red or black, or on a specific number.

In betting, you are basically allocating your resources (chips) in a particular way (choosing odds or evens, red or black, et cetera), with the hope that you will make more money betting on that outcome than on a different one. In business, "resource allocation" means placing or allocating the company's resources in different parts of the business, with the hope of getting a higher rate of return than if you had allocated them in other ways.

When we talk about "sales leadership resource allocation," we're talking about deciding in what areas of sales generation you are going to invest more resources. In order to do this, there are typically a set of rules, a set of odds, and an understandable environment in which you operate. It is much like the game of roulette in that there are certain odds that are understood by everyone at the table, yet there is also an element of luck that you are betting on. You hope that your particular combination of strategy and luck will pay off bigger than that of the others who are playing the game.

In this chapter, I will lay out a number of strategies that will give you an approach for making better resource allocation choices and generating greater returns on your sales effort investments.

Setting the Organizational Understanding of Priority

When we talk about resources, we're not just talking about line items in a budget or in the section called "Approved Expenditures." There are less tangible resources to be allocated as well. People in organizations are always sorting priorities within their individual job descriptions and allocating resources between competing sets of initiatives. This means that there is a certain amount of discretion in where they put their resources–bet to bet, moment to moment, and market situation to market situation. Those people—and they may be in your operations department, marketing department, engineering department, or other areas of the business—look at a sale, or a sales effort, as an interruption of their "regular" work. In their view, they are going to have to stray from their normal activities in order to invest their time and energy in this area called "selling."

Like any new game, selling can be intimidating to those who have not played it before. Imagine you're in Las Vegas, looking at the roulette table for the first time. You're standing just outside of the player's ring. You're watching to try and figure out, "What is my safest bet?" "How do I play this game and not look stupid?" and maybe "Should I even be here?" Often, beginners play either black or red because they can understand that 50:50 ratio of risk. Over time, they may start to try more complex bets. Once they come to understand the game better and become more capable as players, they may make a variety of combinations of bets in a variety of games.

This process is very much like the organization's understanding of the world of selling. At first, they're not certain what the odds really are or what the protocols, guidelines, and rules are, and therefore they enter the game cautiously. That caution shows up in managers and supervisors not investing the right numbers of people in the right ways at the right times in the process. There is often a desire to stay outside of the game and watch the players play a little longer to determine whether or not this is a game in which their contribution has any chance of creating a win.

It is your job as a sales leader to help not just the sales department but the entire organization to understand the game of selling. It is also your responsibility to make certain that others set that game as a priority to be played when asked and not sit on the sidelines, watching the other players and trying to decide whether or not they'll enter the game.

How do you do that?

Share the Hunt

A first step is to post lists of sales targets that are being hunted by the company. This focuses the organization's collective energy and helps people to see these goals as concrete opportunities, and not just some abstract concept of "sales" in the marketplace. Now, nothing will cause operations engineers or others in non-sales jobs to freak out faster than to tell them that they're going to be involved in selling or that they have to make a contribution to a sales process. The first words out of their mouths will be, "I'm not a salesperson." That may be so, but that doesn't mean that the organization doesn't need them to have a fundamental understanding of the sales process and how their work contributes to it. By putting real targets up on the wall, you can make sales a focal point and help people to see that they are participating in a real effort.

One organization we worked with used a detailed outline of a sales process to spur collective motivation. The organization was involved in market research, and the majority of its employees were analysts and PhDs engaged in market research and market research technologies. They did not see themselves as salespeople, nor did they see themselves as relevant to the sales process. In order to generate interest in the sales process, a graphic was mounted in poster-like fashion in the break room. There were seven large banners, each representing a different phase in the sales process. The logo of each company the organization was hunting was posted in whatever phase had been reached to date in the sales process.

As the scientists and analysts came in to get their morning coffee, they would look at the logos on the wall in the various stages of the sales process and begin to ask themselves questions, perhaps including:

- I know someone at that company—could that help?
- I worked at that company—should I tell the sales director about it?
- Why has this particular company been stuck so long in this particular part of our sales process?

Back at their desks, they would e-mail some member of the sales team and ask these and other questions. As they started to understand how the sales process worked and what companies were involved, they began to see themselves as having the potential to contribute. Perhaps they had a connection to a former colleague or to someone they had met at a trade show; perhaps they knew some important market information that had just been published in a trade journal, et cetera. Because of these contributions, the organization as a whole now saw itself as a hunting organization.

Transparency, including relevant updates on sales progress, has the dual power of helping to increase organizational understanding about sales and setting a priority on hunting. Included in the poster example above, by the way, were those sales opportunities that management had decided should not be pursued. This gave confidence to the employees that not every deal would be indiscriminately hunted to just land another piece of business. It also gave them confidence that the sales being hunted had met some criteria about how they would advance the organization and be in line with the company's values. It is very important that you as a sales leader help your organization to understand not only that you've landed a deal or how you've landed a deal, but why you hunted that deal in the first place.

Get Everyone Involved

As the senior sales leader in your organization, you can have an enormous impact on employees who are not traditional salespeople by giving them declared positional responsibilities. Now, here's a secret: if you want to get their engagement, never tell them that they are selling! But if they see themselves as a part of the sales process during which they're going to be asked to use their significant expertise and informational authority to help make a contribution, then their interest goes up. People who are not in traditional sales roles need to see their contribution as being relevant to their expertise, not that they are selling something. A good rule of thumb is to focus on how your organization is solving problems for other companies. By identifying how different members or departments in the organization make a worthwhile contribution, you are helping to improve the organizational understanding that everyone must be involved in various stages of selling in order to land a new account.

Set Thresholds

I once ran an organization that was growing very, very rapidly and landing very large accounts. It was a high-transaction volume business, which means that there was low margin per transaction. In order to make best use of my time as the president and CEO of that company, we set up the following thresholds, or governances:

If the opportunity was worth one million dollars in new revenue to the company, then the sales representative could travel to that account and spend time there to try to sell the account. If that account came to our city to meet with our people and to tour our facilities, then the head of sales and marketing would attend to that person during his or her visit. As CEO, I would stop by, say hello, meet and greet, and leave.

For a two million-dollar account, the vice president of sales and marketing would travel with the sales representative to that company's town. If representatives of that company came to our town, then I would entertain the account and its leaders while they were in town and spend time with them to understand their problems and issues and assist them in understanding our business and how we might be of value.

For a three million-dollar opportunity, not only would I travel to the account's town, but it is also very likely that I would wash their car, take their dog for a walk, and entertain them for dinner. Obviously, I'm exaggerating. But the point is, I didn't travel as the president and CEO for every size deal, and neither should you.

Over time, the organization learned that there were thresholds that would allow for my full investment and participation as the senior sales leader, and there also were thresholds for the vice president and for the salespeople. One result of putting these thresholds in place was that our salespeople went after much, much larger deals. Why? Because if it was a three million-dollar deal, then the likelihood that they would win that deal went up because I was involved.

I don't fool myself; it's not because I'm a remarkable salesperson. But the fact is, once I was involved in that deal as the president and CEO, that deal was of higher value to me, which meant that I would invest more time, energy, and potentially provide a greater amount of creativity in establishing the performance parameters and the final contract. The bigger the deal, the more high-level heads were in the game, and the higher the odds of everyone winning.

Engage personally in opportunities that are truly whale-sized deals for your company. I define a whale as an opportunity that is ten to twenty times the size of your average account. If you are spending time involving yourself in opportunities that are not of this size, you are wasting your time.

Putting thresholds in place can serve a different, but equally important role in an organization with a finite amount of resources that can be invested in any particular new venture. Based upon available equipment, personnel, capital expenditures, facility space, and other factors, thresholding may help determine not only which deals will have the participation of senior executives, but also which deals the organization can handle.

One organization we work with requires a great deal of physical space and equipment for its work. As a result, the executives must carefully consider the pace at which they bring in new deals, the scale of those deals, what the mix of business is, and how they are going to onboard those new accounts. In addition, the company's sales cycle is nine months long and its prospecting cycle is six months long, leading to an overall sales process cycle of as many as fifteen months. Thus, senior executives have to be involved in establishing the thresholds of the deals early in the process so as to make certain that when the opportunity comes on board, there will be available capacity to handle it.

Nothing can be more demoralizing to an organization than to have to say no to business that it fought hard to get because it does not have the available capacity. That looks like bad leadership and bad planning.

Remember That Showing Up Is More Than 90 Percent of the Job

Your leadership in the form of attendance is absolutely paramount. Leading and growing an organization means that you are present at key meetings. A client of ours who owns and runs a 400 million-dollar company participates in the large account strategy sessions. He doesn't always say very much, but everyone knows that he is involved and sees the strategy sessions as valuable. As owner of the company, he often spends a month or two away from the office, traveling or taking care of other investment responsibilities. But he never misses those meetings. His presence sets an important tone in the organization and also aligns with the priority of the company, which is growing and landing more business.

Here's a frequent misunderstanding about leadership and attendance: if you are operating under the belief that selling should be delegated to someone else and not participated in, you are operating under old thinking. In order to demonstrate that you're willing to go the distance with your organization to land business, you must participate on the ground in the actual sales hunts on occasion. Remember, you are only participating in the larger opportunities. Smaller opportunities can be handled by either the threshold structure discussed above or through transaction processing. Here's how that looks:

1. Your participation must be regular, rigorous, and applied to the review of the sales process and to each of your key deals.
2. The participation of your executive management should occur in the same meeting you are in. That's right. They have to be there as a part of a regular review meeting.

3. Whether that meeting is monthly, weekly, or quarterly, you must be part of the discussion about what deals your organization is hunting, what stage of the hunt the team is in, and what resources are needed to land the deal and onboard the business.
4. The annual setting of sales goals for the year or for a particular period is done by an executive management team. It is not a byproduct of the budgeting and projections process. We're playing in a new economy by a new set of rules; therefore, we have to follow a new set of procedures.
5. Sales and revenue management is now an executive management team responsibility; not just a positional function. Organizations that get this right by involving their executive management team are not caught by surprise when opportunities come their way. They also already have buy-in so that they can accelerate the onboarding of new revenue opportunities.

Decide When More is Needed

If you're familiar with baseball, you know that from time to time in a game when things are not going well for the pitcher—when the opposing team is scoring too many runs or getting too many players on base—the coach has to pull a new pitcher from the bullpen. Similarly, in sales, you as the sales leader have to decide when your team needs to do something more than what it's been doing, in order to win the sale.

Data can sound a warning. There's a reason why I say that time kills all deals. That's because it's true. Deals that are stuck, that are bogging down in negotiations, or that seem to be going nowhere are good indicators that it is time to do something new.

Why can't you just rely on feedback from your team? Because often, middle-level management and frontline salespeople in your organization see false positives, which can fool or mislead them. Besides, salespeople tend to be pathological optimists, believing that things are going well with all the deals they're working on. It's also not so easy to come to the boss with a problem, in case it might reflect poorly on them. That's why you as sales leader have the responsibility to see past false positives and make decisions to do something new, which often means more. Now, what does "more" mean?

More Expertise

If your client or prospect is asking for additional information after receiving information that traditionally has been sufficient, this is an indication that your client does not trust the expertise that has been provided so far.

You may need to provide additional expertise from internal or external resources in order to give your client greater confidence. We do this in our personal lives when we seek a second or third opinion about a medical diagnosis or procedure, or when we go to buy a car and bring a trusted friend or loved one with us who has more experience with the process.

This seeking of additional expertise is not unusual, and it happens with increasing frequency in the uncharted world of sales. Your job is to figure out when more expertise is necessary and to make certain that the resources are allocated to obtain that expertise.

More References

Being stalled or stuck can be a function of confidence. Your prospect is weighing the risk of choosing to work with you, choosing a different solution, or doing nothing. Imagine those options on the boardroom table. The decision makers sitting at the table will have varying questions, but all will have one question in common: everyone will want to know how much confidence there is in the potential success of the presented options. References are clearly a vital part of representing your potential success. Sometimes you need to bring more of them to the table if the deal is stalling. However, remember that references are like your savings: be careful how you use them, and realize that once you've used them, they are gone for a period of time.

You can't just use the same reference over and over again because you'll wear out the reference and wear out your welcome. Also, you have to tailor the right reference to the right situation. If you let salespeople use your best references left and right, they'll waste those references when in fact some other sales technique or some other kind of resource would be more appropriate. It's your responsibility to decide when to use some of your best references in the marketplace to give greater confidence to your buyers.

More Energy

I'm surprised how often, when surveyed, buyers say that the reason they went with a particular company was that it "showed more energy." What does that mean? Often it shows up as a certain level of intensity, a speed of response, or attention to detail. All of these demonstrate that your organization is completely committed to and excited about the opportunity.

The easiest and cheapest way to show more energy to your customer is speed. When you are faster in your follow-up notes after a meeting, in your response to a query, in your bid or proposal, all of these show that you are giving more energy and focus than someone else is. You're communicating that your customer is important and will be important after the business is awarded. If you want to know whether more energy is necessary in your organization's sales process, look for the following symptoms:

- Prospects delaying or rescheduling meetings with your salespeople at the last minute
- Meetings with prospects becoming shorter than the norm
- Poor attendance at meetings on the part of buyers from the prospect organization
- Longer delays between communications with people who had traditionally talked to your organization regularly

All of these indicators show that the deal is slowing down and that it's possible that your people may need to exert more energy.

More Commitment

You know that your prospect's commitment is starting to slip when you start to see a deteriorating level of people, as defined by position, slide into your sessions and you get the feeling that the deal is being delegated downstream.

If this happens to you, you're not alone. Nearly two-thirds of B2B marketers identified engaging key decision makers as their top challenge (Johnson 2014).

Downgrading the level of those involved in the process typically shows that the buyer's commitment is diminishing. You need to respond to this development. Show more commitment: elevating the level of people who are participating from your side of the organization and increasing the amount of energy that you're exerting in order to secure the buyer's commitment.

More Money

That's right! More money. It costs money to hunt deals. One of the companies we worked with spends about $250,000 on every large-opportunity response. I'm not talking about throwing money mindlessly at the process. I'm talking about a strategic and appropriate allocation of funds that could include demonstrations, drawings, prototypes, travel and entertainment, and other types of sales efforts and techniques.

It sometimes happens that you are losing in a deal because you are being outspent by a competitor, even though the margin justifies the expenditure. So, why are you spending less? Simple: you don't have the confidence that you're going to win the deal. If you did, you'd spend the money because you'd know you're going to get the money back. It's at times like these when only you as the leader can make the call: "Do we have enough confidence to invest more?" Sometimes in business we borrow a term from blackjack to describe this: "doubling down."

Recently, a client of ours was working on a very, very large opportunity and spending hundreds of thousands of dollars to win this deal. Where was the money coming from? Well, I can tell you right now that it wasn't in the budget. If it's not in the budget, it means that money has to be reallocated from other areas or other budgets. That's why deciding to use more money requires your leadership. Middle-level and lower-level staff do not have access to a flexible budget, nor do they have the broader perspective to weigh potential expenditures against potential gains. Only the organization's leader has that—or should.

Determining When Outside Help Is Necessary

In the past, companies often were very guarded and even a bit arrogant about their approach to landing business in the marketplace. They wanted to go it alone because they thought that they were better than other companies or that other companies would "mess it up." But in the new world of sales, the fact is that alliances, partnerships, supplier relationships, vendor relationships, outside consultants, and other kinds of resources are necessary for landing various kinds of business. Why? Because, in order to be successful and effective, organizations have often specialized, and if they want to win bigger pieces of business, organizations with complementary specialties need to join forces to present a dynamic, confidence-inspiring package to the buying organization.

For example, over the years, I have bought lots and lots of printing solutions. In the early days, the sales rep or the sales rep and a technician from the printing company would show up to present the benefits of different pieces of equipment. Not anymore. The last time we changed our printing solution, five people showed up. One was a network specialist dealing with the internal communication structure of our organization. One was an equipment specialist. One was a service technician. One was our account manager. I'm not sure what the fifth person did—maybe his job was to drive.

Not only did we have five people in the room compared to one or two, but only two of them worked for the same company. The rest were participants from outside of the print solution company's own walls and on the payrolls of their suppliers and partners. Because they brought all those resources to my doorstep on that sales call, they got the job. We knew that we had the right experts in the room doing the right kinds of things, and for that reason, our confidence went up.

I know that it can be tricky to use consultants, vendors, suppliers, and other kinds of outside partnerships. It is your job as the sales leader to facilitate those relationships, determine when they are necessary, and provide parameters under which they will operate effectively.

Betting on Yourself

I often tell people that I don't bet in Vegas, which is true. I don't even put a dollar in a slot machine. The reason is simple. I play for a lot bigger stakes with better odds. The game I play is called "entrepreneurism." Call it what you will. The fact is, at the executive level, you are spending real money in this real-life game we call the marketplace, shifting your chips from place to place to see if you can find the winning combination and get a better return than your competitors.

When you consider the ideas presented in this chapter, perhaps you'll come to the conclusion that you are doing well. If so, I say, "well done." If you are less confident in your self-appraisal, I would tell you that the number-one challenge senior executives have in this changed world of selling is the challenge of leading from the front. I'm not just talking here about being in the closing meetings—most senior executives like that stage in the selling process. I'm talking about making the many resource tradeoff decisions along the way. That's where a leader's absence is felt. In most cases, it is not fear that keeps leaders from taking this course. It is a sense of appropriateness. They have hired sales leaders and therefore they want to empower them to make the choices and not micro-manage. I believe that when it comes to leading your organization through significant change, these thoughts are misguided. Your leaders can do a good job of leading a defined mission and managing a clearly articulated system. But real change must be designed by you and implemented from the top in order to take hold.

Chapter 5: Determining When to Change Course

You've probably already figured this out, but this world that we're selling in is in flux. Things don't stay steady the way they did in the past. This is actually a good thing. When we were locked out of sales opportunities with companies in the past, that usually meant we were locked out for years because things were pretty static in the decision making body or in the needs of their particular business, or because of longstanding relationships they had with prior vendors or suppliers. Today, things are more fluid. That can mean more opportunity. But it also can be rough, because it's hard to predict the future when the future is constantly one big swirling mess of new data, new players, new information, and new market pressures.

That's why it's important for you as a sales leader to understand when to change course. It used to be possible to set a course on a three-year plan, with an annual redo or reboot. That's often no longer possible. You're going to have to get comfortable with a different pace. In today's new selling world, we need to reset our idea of "normal speed."

What's driving change at this insane rate? Technology is a villain we love to accuse. Regulation is accelerating, too—another favorite villain. The speed of information transfer through the digital conduits is another factor. These and more are all in play. In a world driven at a digital pace, the speed of every component of sales must increase. It's one more reason why sales leadership must be at the front of the line for data capture and evaluation.

You also need to create an adaptive environment for dealing with all the data that's coming in. It starts with data capture and making certain that you have the reconnaissance and information necessary, as discussed earlier in this book. You also need to be reframing the operating environment more frequently to make certain that your marketing strategies, sales approaches, and solutions are still relevant and keeping pace with the marketplace.

Determining when to change course is your responsibility. Sales managers and frontline salespeople can give you a lot of data and support for your ideas, but deciding precisely how and when to make the big move rides on your shoulders. If you have to send out for a survey or a market study because you don't have the data you need, chances are you're already behind the curve. You'd be wiser to set up a net to catch significant and relevant marketplace data as it comes in, rather than do semi-annual market surveys.

Establishing a Learning Culture

Establishing that net lets you develop what I would refer to as a learning culture. Often when people talk about learning cultures and learning organizations, it sounds to me like a lot of business pop-culture fluff. But the fact is that repeatedly assessing your customers, prospects, markets, competitors, technologies, and market disruptions will put you in a better position to look at the data in real time and determine more quickly whether or not you need to change course.

Your organization becomes a learning culture, first and foremost, when it knows what to look for in that data. Just as teaching someone how to use the library, the Internet, or a particular knowledge management tool makes him or her more powerful, so establishing an efficient model for assessing marketplace changes makes an organization more powerful.

Walking Away

Sales opportunities can have a certain vortex quality: the more you commit in time, people, and resources, the faster the whirlpool spins, sucking you and your organization toward a conclusion that you may not want, such as, "We're hunting this deal even though we know we are not going to win," or "If we win, it won't be to our best advantage to have won the business."

The longer the process goes on, the more committed people become to staying the course, even if they know that the path will lead them over a cliff. It's crazy, yes, but it's just the nature of being involved in a sales opportunity—unless sales leadership says it's time to walk away. Understand this: no one on your team is going to say "No" if they think you are pushing for "Yes." Your job has to include the willingness to walk away from bad business when you see it.

Setting a Course Is Different from Navigating a Storm

Setting a course entails logistics, strategy, and other components of planning. You have to establish where you are going and how you will measure your progress along the way. You have to put someone in the crow's nest to look for signs of trouble, be it bad weather or a marauding competitor. In contrast, navigating a storm is like being in a fistfight. It's about surviving moment to moment until you reach a period of peace, when the winds have calmed and the waters have stilled.

Sales leaders have to be good at both setting courses and navigating storms. These aren't things you can delegate to management or to the front line; rather, they are the core purpose of leadership. When you change course, you are saying, "We have new objectives, a new understanding of the market conditions. The situation will not go away if we just ignore it."

Changing course isn't something to be done lightly, but when it is done, it must be done with clarity and conviction. It's also important to set your course with care, because too many changes of course can indicate that you have not done adequate reconnaissance, and that can undermine your credibility with your crew.

When the storms come, as they will, an experienced course-setter will be better at spotting and navigating them.

Making the Last Word Choices

Recently, one of my clients went through a very difficult period in which she realized that her industry was changing at such a rapid pace that if her organization had continued on its current course, it would eventually become obsolete and might go out of business. She had envisioned that these industry changes would occur eighteen to thirty-six months in the future, but they had come a lot sooner. She had to rededicate the business in a new direction entirely and invest new capital in order to be prepared. She could seek data, opinions, and information from the people within her organization, but I have noticed that when leaders do this, often what they get from these internal discussions is nothing but incrementalism.

It's interesting that when a company has to dramatically change what it is, what it does, and whom it serves, lots of folks in the organization declare, "We should do something new." But none of them want to do it! Breaking out of the standard ways of doing business to build a new model for the business itself is the job of the sales leader. If you are reading this book, more than likely you carry that responsibility.

The tendency is to stick to the course you're on, making only minor modifications. Sales leaders must understand that they must go outside of themselves into the marketplace to trusted advisors in order to get the data and information necessary to chart a new, transformational approach. At the end of all the discussions, meetings, data analysis, and hand wringing, you are the ultimate decision maker about what happens. These are called "last word choices," because in fact, yours is the last word.

Sales Leadership is about being out on front lines, responding quickly to an ever-changing marketplace with confidence and information. Keep in mind, however, that the information will often be flowing a little slower than you'd like, because of the speed with which you must act.

That's why the new world of selling requires bold leadership on your part, to set the course for your organization and respond with intelligence and daring to changes occurring across the marketplace. If you set yourself up with a learning culture, a more rapid cycle time, and an expectation that change inside your business is not a matter of "if" but rather of "when," you may be in a good position to take advantages where you find them.

So, you have the weather indicators for when to make transformational change. That's the starter's gun for when. This next chapter tells you how.

Chapter 6: Leading Transformational Change

We've been talking about how important it is for business leaders to have data that will help them analyze market indicators and determine what to do next. Pilots rely on instrument panels to provide moment-to-moment information about environmental factors such as temperature, wind speed, and so on, as well as data about the performance of the aircraft. Using their instruments, they can fly safely even in the dark or in heavy fog.

What would a sales leadership instrument panel look like? Before we dig into that, let's talk about a few supporting ideas.

Idea #1: The Most Important Information Doesn't Always Make Sense

When it's dark outside and you're flying by instruments alone, there's something beyond just the data that comes into play as you try to steer your plane differently from your competitors in the marketplace. Some call it "intuition," "experience," or "luck." Whatever it is, it enables you to look at data and information in a way that others do not. This is part of what makes you unique as a leader.

Some of the most important information you'll receive is information that varies from expectation, trajectory, or trend that you have been following. Maybe the trend continues longer than you expect, or you start to see unprecedented variations that you can't make sense of. When you see this type of deviation from expectation, it's an important indicator that needs investigation.

What does investigation entail? It entails drilling down to the deepest level you can on the information to find out what it's really telling you. In the world of Six Sigma, this is the value of asking the question, "Why?" five times before you come to a conclusion. The idea is that the first, second, and third whys will only give you layers of the onion, when what you need to do is get to the root cause.

These variations I'm talking about may be small and seemingly random. They may signify temporary turbulence, or they may be the first rumblings of a major storm on the horizon. If you want to be successful as a sales leader, you have to be willing to dig down and get your fingers in the data itself once you see a variation. The best digital data analysis systems let you do that drilldown on a click-by-click basis. You should be able to drill into any given deal, a given sales leader, or a specific market category. You are looking for new patterns and new information that may lead you to new conclusions.

Idea #2: How to Trust and Verify

Ronald Reagan is famous for saying that when negotiating with the Russians, it was important to be able to trust his negotiating partners, but also to be able to verify the data. Pure trust (or, for that matter, pure doubt) was less effective. For us in the world of sales, the idea of making decisions just on the basis of reading a CRM system or a sales activity tracking report is rather foolish. I often say in my presentations that the world of sales is filled with failed novelists. That's because novelists are fiction writers, and many sales activity reports and CRM documents contain more than a little fiction.

People writing material that others will read tend to write it in such a way as to please the reader and also to cast themselves in the best possible light. That's what salespeople do when they record information in a CRM or sales activity tracking system. Your responsibility as a leader is not only to ensure that there's a culture of accountability and personal integrity in your organization, but also that there is a periodic verification cycle to make certain that these records are being completed accurately and with relevant and appropriate data.

Trust and verification fall into three categories:

1. Sampling. Periodically taking a deep sample of the data that has been provided by the salespeople in your organization can help you understand, verify, and test the accuracy of what is reported in the CRM and sales activity. Dig down into a critical account and look at all of the pieces—

not just the top-level report, but all of the activity and documentation supporting it.

2. Questioning. Meeting with team members and asking them to provide you with an oral report on the status of a particular account, without advance notice and without using notes, gives you an understanding of their level of comprehension of that particular sale or account. Don't feel badly about doing this, as if you're putting these folks on the spot. It's quite natural and to be expected that at one point or another in the overall sales process, a salesperson or contributing party is going to have to describe and discuss what is going on in a given sales process. After all, you have established a step-by-step sales process, with roles and responsibilities for various individuals, and as part of the process you need to gather information and share information with the team or with the prospect. It's entirely appropriate that the key lead on that account be able, without rehearsal or notes, to describe and discuss everything that's been going on over the past two to four weeks with that account, whether one-on-on one with you, or in front of a group of people who are participating in that hunt. That oral report reveals to you not only what is going on in the account and the key lead's command of the issues, but also tells what is being communicated to people who are not necessarily reading the entire CRM or sales activity report. Oral reporting and oral discussion are great ways to learn how your sales people really think about the account and can bring to light important information about the sales process that numerical and digital status reports cannot provide.

3. Auditing the manager. In every sales organization, there are going to be high-priority, mid-priority and low-priority accounts. Your manager should be invested in those high-priority accounts. This means having a working knowledge at all times of the top five to fifteen accounts across the board for his or her territory and all of his or her sales representatives. If your manager has this information, then in a meeting or one-on-one session, you should be able to ask a series of questions about what is going on with certain accounts and the manager's answers should align with what is recorded in your CRM or sales activity panel. Auditing the manager provides you with a clear understanding of your sales management team's priorities. It reveals the sales manager's expectations and handling of the salespeople. It is always appropriate to do an audit of management as part of your sales leadership to ensure that the culture you are building of detail orientation, information exchange, and process adherence is being followed.

Too many organizations have leaders who watch their sales activities from afar, never dirtying their hands in the real work that is occurring in the marketplace except for the very, very biggest of deals, and only participating at the very end near the closing. If you want to be a successful sales leader, you need to be prepared to trust and verify, at any given point in the sales process, on any account, whenever you decide it is necessary—and your sales team needs to know that you can and will dive in that deep.

Idea #3: How to Forecast the Future

Historians like to say that the future can be predicted by looking at the past. I am not certain that's valid anymore. The vast changes in communication, the pressure for urgency, the increasingly competitive environment, and other drivers are making a detailed examination of the past less and less relevant in planning business strategy for the future. But as the leader, your job is to help define what is possible. In order to do that, you must attempt to define the future. I'm not talking about tarot cards or tea leaves here. Actually, you can use something you already have: your instrument panel. It should provide some important indicators about the future. So, what should you be looking for?

First, look for the trends. Trends are not just conversion rates, the size of the average deal, or negotiation patterns and margin rates. Rather, you need to be looking at the following:

1. Competitors' performance
2. Delays in the deal caused by negotiating strategies
3. Pricing challenges
4. Modifications to specifications required for product or service offerings
5. Changes in who is part of the buyer's table

6. Internal delays caused by your own staff or resources

If you want to predict the future, look at variation in these trends over a brief window of time—I normally look at no more than ninety days in the near past—to determine if in fact you are starting to see changes in your data as represented by these factors in your sales process.

Also, assess the five engagement gauges of your sales process (discussed in depth in Chapter 8) to see if things are moving as expected:

1. Your people
2. Their people
3. Your information
4. Their information
5. Cycle Time

You can determine what challenges you will face in the future based upon what data is appearing or not appearing, what people are appearing or not appearing, and what delays you are experiencing in your sales process. The great benefit of forecasting the future in this way is that you are also simultaneously auditing your sales process, spotting problems, making adjustments, and tuning up your process to align with what you see on the horizon.

By having this information available to you on your Instrument Panel, you will start to see the shape of the future in the form of very early indicators of sales resistance and success.

Looking Toward the Future: How to Create Explosive Growth

Businesses develop along a series of set points and set point changes. At each set point, the organization adjusts its pace, people, processes, measures, and systems—first to arrive at the new set point, and then to sustain that set point.

Want your business to find a new set point? Here's a roadmap to follow.

1. Define your new set point by size, pace, volume, accounts, et cetera. For most companies, you can calculate a new set point by doubling your current growth rate. But that's just a guideline. What you are really trying to achieve is a new business operating level that requires measurable improvement across your operating and sales organizations.

2. Pick your set point timing. Entrepreneurs don't usually have the attention span for a sustained effort. So aim to achieve the new set point in less than twelve months–the shorter the change cycle, the better for you.

3. Determine and execute needed changes. In one of the businesses that I ran, we had a set-point change that required accelerating a new facility ramp-up: A seven-month plan got shaved down to thirty days. It took very hard work in planning, vendor sourcing, staffing, and other disciplines–but changing that set point for our business transformed our growth curve. Executing the changes was painful, but all future steps became remarkably easier.

4. Set a different change tempo. As the example above shows, some drastic measures may be needed in order to change your set point. But once you are at the new level, you won't need the same level of dramatic life change to stay there.

5. Rinse and repeat. Expect a stair-step pattern: Reset your set points, attain them, and then start the process again. So, prepare yourself to revisit this cycle.

Leadership during transformational change is not magic, but some parts of it are more magic than science.

Part 2: Sales Management

Introduction

When I work with sales executives, typically VPs and senior managers, I usually find that the people in these positions are poorly skill-balanced for the job. They are strong in one or two areas and weak in the other one or two others.

Let me explain. I find that the sales executive position is really a mash-up of three different roles, each having different responsibilities:

- **Salesperson:** Close the big opportunities, develop customer relationships, grow strategic accounts, solve customer problems
- **Administrator:** Handle hiring, compensation, policy compliance, budgeting, and forecasting
- **Developer:** Create strategy. Teach, coach, motivate, and discipline staff every day to attain performance

In professional football, this would be similar to holding the positions of general manager, coach, and quarterback simultaneously. It's not only the amount of work that makes the role difficult; it's also the breadth of skills required to perform all roles well.

Because two of these roles, salesperson and developer, on paper, have many similar experiential qualities, it is understandable why high performers in the roles of sales are promoted so frequently into leadership positions. But add in that third role—administrator—and it becomes evident why so many underperform or fail. Unlike other promotion ladders, moving into a sales leadership role is not just a matter of doing similar work at an increased scale. It is very different work at a very different scale.

The sales leaders I work with want to spend most of their time in strategy development, closing big opportunities, and coaching. When describing how their time is spent, however, few describe doing that work. "Administrivia," ceaseless reporting requirements, procedural compliance, and troubleshooting are all at the top of the list of time-takers.

Will the new world of selling be better for the beleaguered leaders of the sales teams in terms of what they do and how much of their time is spent doing it?

The bad news is that many of the challenges of the three roles are the same. The good news is that in this new world of selling, if you're a sales leader, you will be able to spend more of your time doing what sales leaders tell us are the favorite parts of their job. It's about changing from high-time/low-yield activities to high-yield activities. Making that shift is about shifting your leverage.

In Part 2, we'll focus on leverage in these areas:

- **Competitors:** Being a step ahead of the competition always gives you an advantage. Being ahead of your industry gives you a chance for market share grab. By knowing and taking advantage of the trends that are reshaping the way selling and revenue generation happen, you leapfrog over the slower-moving players.
- **Systems:** Streamlining planning and managing functions into efficient systems frees you as a manager to focus on assessing the information you're getting from the field and using that information to make the best possible next move—rather than spending your time trying to get the information.
- **People:** You have to pick winners to manage winners. And just hiring winners is no longer enough—they are not going to "figure it out on their own." The game has gotten more complicated, so you are going to have to coach well and fast.

Because the world of selling has changed, your focus has to change.

Chapter 7: The Three Trends of Sales

If you are in a sales leadership role, then sales are all you think about, because you and your team are expected to land them to keep your job, to grow your division, department, or territory, and to ultimately grow the company.

There was a time when selling was simple—not easy, but simple. There was just a handful of things you needed to do right:

- You needed salespeople who could build and keep relationships over time.
- You needed a sales team that wanted to work hard and hustle.
- You needed to make sure that you had geographic coverage and market coverage, and that you were hitting enough of your key prospects frequently enough to keep those relationships going.
- You needed to articulate a unique value proposition to set you apart from your competitors in the marketplace.

That was it. Simple. Not easy, but simple.

Why did you stick to this model? Because it worked. It brought in the sales you needed and added new customers at a regular pace. You didn't need to change it, so you didn't.

Now, one fundamental truth of selling is that sales processes don't change until buying processes do. That's because salespeople do those things that work. When they find that the work that they're doing isn't getting the results that they want, they change, albeit a little slower than you might like. Maybe that's what's happening in your company right now. Or maybe you've noticed that despite all the energy you've been putting into your selling process, you're getting less back. There are some reasons for that.

Trend #1: Margin Pressure

The economic changes that are happening in the marketplace are caused by many factors, including high competition. What's happening right now is probably that you're feeling a commoditization of your product or service in the marketplace. That pressure is starting to squeeze out the margins you once had. Fundamentally, you're not able to provide the same level of commission to salespeople for small transactions. You're needing to make larger and larger transactions just to stay where you are.

Trend #2: More Power to the Buyer

We selling organizations used to have a lot more power than our buyers did. We knew more than they did about the features and benefits of the products and services in the marketplace. We knew more than they did about our competitors. We had the power that came with knowledge.

That has vanished with the rise of the Internet.

Buyers can go online and learn about products and services. They can compare features and pricing. They can even read reviews by other users about your products and services and those of your competitors before they ever meet with you. In the Introduction, I mentioned that 57 percent of the buyer's decision has already been made before meeting with the salesperson. Think about that – 57 percent. If 57 percent of the decision has been made before the buyer contacts you, that means you're already behind the curve when you connect with a prospect, because that prospect has likely already analyzed the options and pricing in the marketplace, researched your competitors' offering, reliability, and stability, and formed an opinion on your company and its offering, reliability, and stability. If you don't change your selling process to keep pace with these changes, your organization can be transformed from one that sells to one that is merely bought from. And you lose control of the process.

Trend #3: The Growth of Compliance

The third trend that changes execution of the buying process is compliance. The Sarbanes-Oxley Act of 2002 was part of a large snowball effect that increased the governance requirements of companies in how they looked at all of their relationships in the marketplace.

One result was that there is a lot more review of business expenditures. Business-related meals, events, and gifts are closely scrutinized. As a result, we no longer have the time and latitude we used to have in which to develop personal relationships with our buyers. Instead, the relationship is governed by procurement and purchasing, compliance, and other groups within our biggest customers. In essence, the message is, "We don't want there to be a personal relationship between the buyer and the seller. We want to keep this an arm's-length transaction."

Governance of the buyer/seller relationship also shows up in bidding and quoting processes such as RFPs and RFQs, in which buyers send what they believe are accurate specifications (though not always the right ones), and then we respond.

Again, who controls the process? The buyer. So, what is our role as salespeople?

Well, there are three swim lanes to look at.

Swim Lane #1: Get Super-Efficient at Transactions

Become the most efficient and effective transaction processor that you can be by creating an efficient, accurate, timely, and cost-effective way for customers to process individual transactions. That's typically done online, through a portal, through some sort of a store or store environment, or through one of your inside salespeople. In this process, you are valued not for your salesperson's knowledge, but for how quickly, accurately, and cost-effectively you can provide value.

Swim Lane #2: Become an Outstanding Buying Processor

This really means facilitating the buyer's selection process. It's about your organization's ability to respond to the buyer's RFP, RFQ, or bid or quote process accurately, completely, in a detailed fashion, and in compliance with the buyer's process. You aren't really selling so much as facilitating the client's buying process by doing the best you can to be responsive, cost-effective, and in compliance with the rules and responsibilities the client has laid out.

Swim Lane #3: Take Back the Selling Process

You can still own and drive the selling process, but if you want to go this route, there are three key things you have to recognize.

First, if you're going to play in this bigger arena, you have to solve bigger problems—the kind of systemic, organizational problems that affect the overall output of your customer's business. These are the issues you will need to identify and address in your selling.

Secondly, if you're going to be taking on problems of that size, you have to be talking to people higher up the food chain, because those are the people responsible for solving bigger problems. That means you'll need a methodology for getting to those people.

Third, you have to get used to having more people on both sides of the table. On their side, they'll want their subject matter experts present—their IT people, supply chain management people, enterprise resource planning people, operations people, and so on. And they won't want to talk just to your salesperson. They'll want to talk to their peers in terms of rank and expertise. So, you'll need to bring a tableful of people to the conversation in order to land those much larger opportunities that are out there.

As you've probably figured out, if you're in Swim Lane #1, you're dealing with smaller-sized purchases. In Swim Lane #2, facilitating the buying process, you'll find mid-sized opportunities. The biggest opportunities are where you really have control of selling, but you have to step up big in order to get them.

Consider which of these swim lanes you want to operate in. Do you want to operate in the transaction processing swim lane, where you make sure that you are more effective, more efficient and more accurate? Do you want to be in the buying process swim lane, which means you're better and more effective at responding at the RFPs and RFQs and other proposal documents submitted to your organization? Or do you want to be more focused on the selling process, talking to larger organizations, higher-ranking people, and more people, about bigger problems?

In my experience, based on having run four fast-growth organizations, you can choose one, maybe two, swim lanes, but you can't choose all three. If you try to be everything to everyone, you won't be enough of anything to anyone. So, what will it be? The clock is ticking. The world has changed its buying process, and you must change your selling process. Go out and grow your business. Choose your swim lanes. Then execute flawlessly.

Chapter 8: Managing the Selling Process

In the past, salespeople had a fair amount of control over their selling process. They were given a territory, a pricing structure, a margin target, and a set of products and services that they could offer. They were responsible for managing their territory and producing results. Sales management provided oversight, facilitated requests back to the corporate offices to ensure that orders were expedited, and generally stayed out of the way. There was additional work with salespeople who were unproductive, (including moving them out of the system if they didn't improve), and in coaching and developing those who were new to the system. The hope was that they would become proficient at operating profitably and would not need nearly as much support in the future as they did when they were being trained.

That's how things used to be. Now, the role of sales management is much different.

Salespeople do not own their territories, customers, prospects, or product lines—the company does. It is now your role as sales manager to view their territories, customers, and products as if assessing a financial portfolio that you are responsible for investing. The people involved, the marketing dollars spent, and the efforts expended are all for you to decide. It is your responsibility to make your investments wisely. Since the time and attention of your salespeople are part of that investment, it is your responsibility to own their calendar, their workflow, and where they spend their time.

This may seem like sacrilege, or you may be of the old mindset that this is micromanagement. But in today's marketplace, the investment belongs to the company, not the sales rep. In the old world, sales representatives were involved in transaction processing, running from customer to customer to pick up orders and to see if there was "anything else we can do to help you out." In the new world, transaction processing is handled by online digital means or by toll-free calls. In the old world, sales reps kept their ears to the ground to find out if a new RFP, a new project, or a new opportunity was coming in. In the new world, those opportunities are generated through purchasing, procurement, or some sort of public bid.

What does that leave for the world of selling? It leaves sales management in the role of picking targets for their salespeople to do reconnaissance, developing a point of access, and securing new Executive Sponsor meetings, (we'll discuss Executive Sponsors in more detail in later chapters), so that a team can participate in a sales process.

Notice I used the word "team" just now. Sales in the old world hinged on the actions of just two people: the buyer and the seller. The new world does not operate like that for the reasons I've already described. And so, as a sales manager, you are now responsible for directing the efforts of a response team.

To summarize, your new responsibilities as a Sales Manager include:

1. Selecting targets. Working with sales leadership, you must establish a filter that helps to define the most likely candidates for higher-opportunity sales efforts.

2. Defining priorities. It is then your responsibility to direct your salespeople toward the high-opportunity candidates they should be chasing, in what order, and with what amount of effort and time. There's an old adage that salespeople talk to whomever will talk to them. In the new world, your responsibility is to make certain that they are talking to those organizations and individuals who have much larger opportunities that may come to fruition in the very near future. Talking about some vague opportunity that may or may not occur a year or two from now is a waste of time. Good sales managers keep those opportunities that are real and relevant to the current circumstances in the crosshairs of their salespeople.

3. Defining time guidelines. Once you recognize that a salesperson's time is no longer his or her own, but actually a representation of the company's investment in the marketplace, then it is your responsibility to set and enforce guidelines for how each of your salespeople spends his or her time. They no longer can just meander about a territory or go on a sweep of their current account base with the intention of "checking in and finding out what's going on." Rather, they must undertake a strategic and surgical approach to pursuing identified targets in a prescribed way.

4. **Monitoring compliance.** Consistency in executing a sales process gives the organization valuable data about what is and isn't working. We're not talking about activity management and monitoring for its own sake. You are responsible for gathering data that allows you and other leaders in the organization to monitor what is happening in the marketplace regarding customers, competitors, and surrounding regulations and technologies shifts. When variance against the system starts to become the norm, the data becomes less relevant, and making data-driven adjustments in the organization becomes almost impossible. As a sales manager, you are working toward compliance in the sales process to protect the integrity of the data capture, so that everyone has relevant data for making good decisions going forward.

5. **Walking the path and dealing with the terrain.** Your sales process lays out a map for action, but a map is just a two-dimensional representation of a sequential process. Good sales management also addresses the third dimension: assessing the terrain of what is going on in the marketplace, based on the data you're getting (including variant data) from the sales process. Based on that data, there may be occasions when you'll send out a scouting team of selected salespeople to find out new information. Then it's up to you to analyze what they bring back and use that information to better navigate the terrain.

6. **Escalating for visibility and resources.** There will be occasions when competing priorities of other departments in the organization impede progress on landing a big account. It's your responsibility to make certain that significant sales opportunities are visible to leadership, and to secure from less-than-enthusiastic parties inside your organization the resources needed for a successful sales process.

7. Knowing when (and when not) to expedite. It's your job to expedite what needs to be expedited—and to know when not to. Remember what happened to "the boy who cried wolf"? Similarly, if you try to expedite every opportunity, soon no one will respond. Salespeople are often viewed as that proverbial "boy who cried wolf." For the sake of the organization and for the sake of your reputation and that of your salespeople, you'll need to be the gatekeeper on when an opportunity needs to be expedited, and when everyone should simply follow the normal sales process.

As you can see, managing the sales process in today's new world has a lot to do with analyzing the scene, formulating strategic direction, and then communicating it down the line to the salespeople. It's new and it's complex, but when it works, the triumph is sweet.

The Selling Process

Over the past fifteen to twenty years, automated sales process documentation in the form of CRMs and activity tracking software has made the activities of sales staff more transparent to the organization—or at least, it was supposed to. But some might argue that while management was increasing its measurement of sales activities, salespeople were increasing their fictitious representation of what they were actually doing. The IT expression "garbage in, garbage out" can apply to CRM systems and sales activity tracking systems as much as to any other. In complex sales processes with far-flung sales forces operating in large territories, sales management needs a reliable dashboard of some sort in order to evaluate what's happening in the field, make good decisions based upon that information, and then implement changes and see what happens. In addition, the kind of information that organizations need in order to understand large-account selling activities is different than what it used to be.

In the past, as most of us know, the collection of sales data was based upon a funnel principle: picture a pipeline with a huge, wide mouth at the top that then gradually narrows to a small opening at the bottom. The sales process started with a large number of sales prospects dropping into that wide mouth. Then the funnel would narrow as candidates and opportunities were eliminated by their own choice or by the selling organization. Those that made it to the other end concluded in a sale.

The sales funnel model has been used for more than forty years to describe the process of winnowing out sales prospects from non-sales prospects and also for measuring performance statistics. However, this model lumps together all levels and types of sales: transactional processing sales, sales process compliance sales, and large and complex sales. If you agree that there are three swim lanes for sales (see Chapter 7), then your measurement doesn't have to include all three types of your sales for your management efforts. Rather, you really only need to find out what sales process activities indicate progress on large and complex sales.

In our system, we look at what we refer to as "gauges of engagement" to assess whether progress is actually occurring in a sales process. As a quick refresher, remember that more people from both the buying and the selling organization are involved in the process of complex deals. Complex deals also require higher levels of certainty and a greater amount of information exchanged between the selling and the buying organizations. The core four gauges of engagement to be measured at each stage in an overall sales process are:

1. Your people
2. Their people
3. Your information
4. Their information

Looking at these four gauges, stage by stage as the selling process unfolds, will give you a clearer indication than a funnel model as to the potential success of the deal, based on whether you are giving and receiving the right information, gaining access to the right people, and securing the support and participation of your own subject matter experts at each stage. All of this relevant detail will help you to gauge whether you are winning or losing, and if you're losing, what might be needed to turn the situation around.

In other industries, this model is referred to as a stage-gate process, meaning that at each stage, certain things need to be accomplished before the "gate" at that stage opens, allowing the participant to go to the next stage. The stages or gauges are set according to the type of information needed (for example: the specifications and resources required from both sides in order for the contract to be executed) and the people who need to be involved from both sides at any particular stage (for example: our tech team and their tech team must meet to determine whether our product will work with their current technology system). Once the identified information has been exchanged and the people have met, the gate can open and the selling process can move to the next stage.

One of the key understandings about a stage-gate process is that you cannot move from one stage to the next stage without having accomplished all of the defined elements for the stage you're in. Thus it is a very process-oriented approach and gives a great deal of control and insight into what's really happening in the sales process on an account-by-account, representative-by-representative basis. By establishing identified expectations at each stage along the way, you have set up performance measures that then tell you whether your people need coaching or development in order to complete that stage. This process will also tell you whether the deal is progressing according to plan or whether it is variant to plan. The variants will need investigation, and you may decide to modify your plan based on what the variants reveal. But at least you will know right away where the process is deviating from expectations, and where the greatest number of problems are occurring.

There's a fifth gauge we need to add, and that is the gauge of time. Each stage should be assigned a certain amount of time, or cycle time, in which to show progress. Now, you may be thinking, "Well, it depends, Tom, on what's going on with that particular account." I'm not denying that sales of this size and complexity have their own time frame. They do. However, by setting an outer limit as to the number of weeks any one account should spend in any one stage in the sales process, you'll be able to spot trends that will indicate whether or not you should be concerned about the pace of a particular sale.

By setting up these five gauges for a given prospect—their information, our information, their people, our people, and the cycle time per stage—

you can establish in your dashboard clear indicators of whether you are winning, losing, or being delayed in the sales process. This model and the level of information it yields varies dramatically from the measures we see in typical input/output activity tracking systems. You've probably seen a great deal of tracking around the following measures for sales:

1. Number of leads per day, per week, or per month
2. Number of calls made
3. Number of presentations made
4. Number of new contacts secured
5. Number of proposals submitted

These are what we would refer to as "inputs." They show the kinds of activities that are occurring in a sales process, without really showing true progress. All of these are inputs on the part of sales representative, who is trying to stuff as much activity as possible into the mouth of the funnel in the belief that it will shake down into a certain volume coming out of the end of the funnel.

The outputs for sales reps, of course, included things like:

1. Closed sales
2. Lost sales
3. Size of sale
4. Extended sales
5. Number of contacts achieved

This input/output system is great for simplistic sales. But in complex sales, the process lasts for weeks, maybe even months. These kinds of inputs are not indicative of changes in behavior that you need to make or adjustments to your process that should be facilitated to make your organization more effective in closing more business. As a sales manager, it is your responsibility to make certain that there is adherence to a sales process that captures more relevant data and tracks a more dynamic process. Eighty-three percent of what is tracked is simply recorded (Searcy 2013). This means sales managers are spending an enormous amount of time looking at information in their CRM that is irrelevant to the progress of the process. Simply recording calls or visits where key objectives are not accomplished and no movement to the next stage happens is wasteful both to the reps recording it and to the managers looking at it.

Elsewhere, I've talked about how leaders and managers must look at every aspect of the sales and marketing effort the way an investment banker looks at a portfolio, carefully deciding how and where to make investments based on performance. Your data must reveal what measures your organization is taking, what tools you are offering, who is involved, and how all of these elements are performing (or not) to increase your organization's overall success. By looking at this data over time, you will gain an understanding of whether you are making the right investments, and how you might need to change the mix for a higher return. You will start to see a clearer picture of who is performing well and who is lagging behind, and at which stages their sales efforts are being delayed or accelerated. This gives you the insights needed to coach and develop your sales representatives in their individual contributions. You also have an indication of which tools and messages are working in the overall sales process to bring a higher yield.

This system also helps you tailor performance expectations to each of your sales representatives. New sales representatives are probably going to have to spend more of their time prospecting to establish new Executive Sponsors. Veteran sales representatives are going to spend more of their time meeting with their existing sales accounts and facilitating growth and expansion conversations with the appropriate subject matter experts.

As you introduce new products into your offerings to support older products and services, your performance expectations will change based upon the individual portfolios of individual salespeople out in the marketplace. Because you are now a portfolio manager of resources dedicated to selling, you can move resources around based upon how they perform in an identified and understandable system.

Motion versus Movement

As you think about what kinds of expectations to set for each sales stage that will allow you to be more successful with your sales representatives, consider what we refer to as "motion versus movement."

"Motion" is the term that we use to describe all of the activities that occur in getting people together, having conversations, and exchanging information within a given sales stage. Whether it takes one call or five calls, one meeting or five meetings, one document or twenty documents, it doesn't matter. All of that is motion inside a system. All of the activities that are commonly tracked in input/output measures of the past are really just motion. They don't indicate true productivity. There's a common assumption that if we do more, we will get more. However, the data indicates that the hardest-working individual out there does not necessarily always have the highest yield, belying the theory that activity guarantees result. When it comes to measuring performance, we want to spend less time tracking the number of motions being made, and more time focusing on movement.

"Movement" is the term we use to denote completion of one stage and movement to the next. In a stage-gate process, this means that all the items in one stage have been completed, so the gate opens to the next stage. Movement along a sales process indicates that you are approaching either a close or the elimination of a prospect for lack of a good fit. Over time, there is a normalizing of the overall volume of what happens in your movements. As a sales leader, you will gradually become familiar with the number of movements generally needed to complete a given measurement cycle, which allows you to set expectations person by person as to how many movements they make per measurement cycle.

In my own business, we have done something rather untraditional in coaching companies on how to best manage their sales forces. We have asked them to consider giving a value of "one" to every movement from one stage to the next in the sales process. That's right. Whether you close a deal, move a deal off of the dashboard because you lost it, or add a deal to the dashboard, it doesn't matter. Each one of these additions, subtractions, or progressions has a value of one.

By managing these expectations over time and giving each movement a value of one, you are communicating to your salespeople that this is a process rather than a personal statement about each sales rep's capability. The measurement tool is a statement about the process of "our people" interacting with "their people." It measures the sum total of everyone's efforts, as well as the effectiveness of the selling process as it has been conceived.

We have found that by working with organizations in this way, and using a dashboard that shows movement, rather than motion, we are better able to spend our time focusing on the overall effectiveness of the organization in selling and not be distracted by the individual contribution of one particular salesperson. Renowned management consultant W. E. Deming is famous for saying, "Winning organizations focus on process and losing organizations focus on people." We believe that in the world of sales management, it is wise to embrace the idea that the process is what is to be trusted and modified, and that people are the secondary element to be evaluated for their contribution to the process. Complex systems have more contribution capability than one particular person. By focusing on the process, you as the manager are making the system better as well as creating the opportunity to work with people in your organization to help them hone their unique contribution and make the overall process more effective. When this works, it's a win-win all around.

Chapter 9: Hiring for the New Sales World

Think back on the qualities you used to look for when hiring for sales positions. Your list probably included the following characteristics:

- Charismatic
- Hardworking
- Good presenter
- Networker
- Closer

Aren't those things important in today's new sales world? Of course they are. But because the buying process has changed, they're just not enough anymore. Consider the ways that buying has changed:

1. There are more people involved. For major sales deals, as I've mentioned, there are a lot of people on both sides of the table: specialists, subject matter experts, financial people, analysts, end users, and technology people. No one salesperson can be knowledgeable in all of the necessary areas. Charisma will only get you so far. After that, demonstrated and knowledgeable expertise is what will win the deal.

2. Processes are more structured and require more approvals. Greater governance and other changes in procurement and purchasing mean that buying decisions are influenced less by personal relationships and more by approval chains and compliance components on the Excel spreadsheet. Once again, the effort of a single charismatic sales representative can't by itself prevail. In fact, with increasing frequency there are mechanisms in place to keep the sales representative from ever personally meeting or calling some of the participants in the purchasing process.

3. Competitive and comparative information is available at buyers' fingertips. You don't need one more lecture on the power of the Internet. You've seen it in operation for a full ten to fifteen years as a transforming power in commerce. I will only add here that the good presentation skills of a sales representative have in some ways been supplanted by the videos, white papers, and other materials available online to your buyers in advance of your salesperson meeting with them.

And of course there are also online reviews. It doesn't matter how great a presentation your salesperson can give; if there's a review or an independent evaluation available online, your sales representative is no longer presenting. He or she is either echoing what has been said (if the review is positive), or defending against it (if the review is negative). Either way, your rep's voice is no longer the first voice a prospective buyer will hear.

4. Salespeople have an increased fear of making mistakes. As organizations have flattened out over the last decade or two, there has been a greater sense of fear among workers that they will be terminated. There's an overall sense of: *if I make a mistake, I won't be forgiven and they won't look at it as a learning opportunity. They'll just get rid of me.* This fear dampens the selling spirit and can prevent salespeople from taking the risk of going hard after prospects.

In short, organizations are more reliant on systems, processes, and objective evaluation in making their decisions than they are on the opinions and abilities of just one person. For this reason, charisma, presentation skills, and networking ability are of diminishing value in comparison to other skills. Let's take a look at the skills needed in order to be successful in today's sales process.

Core Skills for the New World of Selling

There are five core skills that sales representatives need in today's new marketplace. If they have these, in addition to the skills mentioned previously, their chances of being successful rise dramatically.

Skill #1: Ability to secure the "Executive Sponsor." The Executive Sponsor is a term I use for the person in the buying organization who:

- Has the authority to sign the contract or purchase order
- Has the problem that your organization can solve

- Can bring the necessary people to the table for the discussion
- Is willing to stay in the loop through the sales process
- Is willing and able to break logjams

Executive Sponsors are those individuals who can push the process forward in the buying organization. The salespeople you need to hire in today's selling world are people who have the skills to secure the commitment of the Executive Sponsors.

If your sales representatives are starting to show a diminishing yield in their accounts, the inability to get and hold the attention of Executive Sponsors is likely the number one reason why. I'll discuss how to secure an Executive Sponsor in more detail in Chapter 12, but let's take a quick look here at the most important abilities a salesperson must have in order to secure an Executive Sponsor:

1. The ability to speak the language of executive buyers. Remember this when looking to have a sales conversation—or any important business conversation: you get sent to whom you sound like. A salesperson who speaks the language of a middle-level buyer or a frontline buyer will be delegated down to that level in the organization and will lose the power accorded by access to an Executive Sponsor. In order to get the attention and secure the commitment of an Executive Sponsor, a salesperson must speak the language of an Executive Sponsor. If the people you are hiring do not have the capability to do that, chances are that they will be unable to learn that skill under your management. You do not need a tutoring project; you need an effective salesperson.

2. The ability to navigate the gatekeepers. Navigating gatekeepers has been a sales skill forever. There's always been a secretary, receptionist, or someone standing in the way of a salesperson getting the eyes or ears of a decision maker. These days, the gatekeepers are also digital and include voicemail and e-mail. A salesperson's ability to navigate around a gatekeeper and get to an Executive Sponsor is critical. The buying process will likely grind to a halt without the energy of an Executive Sponsor pushing it along.

3. The ability to leverage the circumstances. Circumstances in the marketplace change on a regular basis. An effective salesperson has the skills to recognize what is changing the marketplace and how to put it to use. Regulations change, technologies change, and competitors and marketplace pressures are constantly shifting. Effective salespeople incorporate these changes into their communications so skillfully that they're able to use the changes as leverage to capture the attention and secure the momentum of an Executive Sponsor in a buying organization.

4. The ability to do the necessary reconnaissance. Effective sales representatives know how to stay current with all that is going on in the marketplace. By reading blogs and market materials, keeping abreast of current events, and engaging with others in the industry, they always know what is going on with competitors and with changes in market conditions, prospects, and customers.

5. The ability to leverage social media and other nontraditional outreach technologies. Better sales representatives know how to use social media and other outreach technologies to accomplish items 1 through 4, keeping themselves informed, current, and relevant in the marketplace.

There are a lot of people from the old world of selling who are unwilling to be efficient by leveraging the Internet for data. The problem is, they are always a day late and a dollar short in the conversation with an Executive Sponsor, so they are delegated over to procurement or purchasing or down to frontline manager, where all they get are transactional scraps.

Skill #2: Project management and facilitation skills. Project management and facilitation have become primary skills for sales representatives as they manage the details of a complicated sales process involving many people on both sides.

In the past, we would get a secretary or some sort of administrative support for a "rock star" salesperson, because they "can't keep up with the paperwork, but they're worth it." Those days are gone. The fact is that the lone gunman approach to selling without any detail orientation or tolerance level for supporting paperwork is no longer successful, and it has a diminishing rate of return. Today, what's admired in the best salespeople is a collaborative approach and collaborative leadership.

Skill #3: Detail orientation. I've addressed this in part above, but the fact is that everyone is watching in the digital world for your ability to manage the details. Salespeople can't hide behind excuses like "it must have gotten lost in the mail," or "I sent that. I don't know why you didn't get it," or, "It must have gotten delayed in shipping. Let me check it out." No one buys these excuses anymore. The fact is that we can track a shipment of a product or a document instantaneously through online means. Voicemails and e-mails are dated and time-stamped with source codes noting their origins. Project management software shows who is and isn't holding up his or her end of the deal. Not sweating the details compromises the credibility not only of your salesperson, but also of your entire organization. A lack of detail orientation isn't just sloppy; it is terminal.

Skill #4: The ability to work with subject matter experts on both sides of the table. In the past, salespeople got a bad rep for their inability to work with people inside the organization. Rock star salespeople were great at going out and making commitments that operations, engineering, or IT couldn't fulfill; then coming back and throwing temper tantrums to try and get what they wanted.

In the new world, this is no longer acceptable or productive behavior. Because subject matter experts of seller and buyer alike are working together, it becomes paramount that your salespeople be able to work smoothly with your company's team and with the buyer's team as well. In this new world, salespeople become cheerleaders, camp counselors, and encouragers, ensuring that the subject matter experts in their organization are all pulling together toward one end goal.

Skill #5: Passion. One of the oft-cited reasons buyers give for deciding to go with one selling organization over another is the demonstrated and coordinated passion of the sales team.

This is not a dispassionate world, so sales is not only about price. Organizations are looking for a sense of confidence and certainty, and one of the ways that is communicated is through the coordinated passion and commitment of the selling team.

Statistics indicate that the team with that demonstrated passion will win, even if they're selling at a higher price. because their passion gives the buying company the sense that its account will get more attention.

That's why one of the key responsibilities of a sales manager is the ability to generate enthusiasm within your own organization and in all those who represent your company to the customer in the marketplace.

How do you find these diversely skilled and non-traditional sales people? It is expensive to build these skills yourself in sales people. The five key skills presented tell you what you are looking for, but now how to find it. Here are some approaches to interviewing candidates that will give you insights into the new skills necessary for success in sales people.

Performance-Based Interview Questions

Here are a few questions that will help you gauge candidates' sales production potential:

- "Tell me about the first year's new sales revenues you generated in your last position."
- "Tell me about the past year's new sales revenues you generated in your last position."
- "What was the size of the largest sale, the second-largest sale and third-largest sale in each of those two years?"

Why these questions? When I hire salespeople, I'm looking for new sales production potential. Unless they're being hired to take over a productive territory with a minimal requirement for new sales, I want to know what they can produce, not just what they can maintain or grow.

Maxim: Never hire someone expecting that person to sell a deal larger than the largest deal he or she ever sold every day.

Caution: Make certain that the candidate's answer is about new accounts for which he or she has generated initial sales, not new sales to existing customers, or sales growth with existing customers.

Buried in the resume and the dialogue is the truth about actual sales performance. Too many resumes and interviews are focused on total dollars, and not on the breakdown. This is the performance you are hiring for, but you will have to dig to get the information you need.

Sales Cycle Questions

Here are two questions to help determine the type of sales cycle a salesperson will likely excel in:

- "Walk me through the sales cycle and the sales process you followed in your most successful years of selling."
- "When do you stop working on a prospect in the sales cycle?"

When you're trading up, you're not looking for a new sales trainee whom you'll need to bring up to speed. You want a producer who will assimilate easily and quickly into your system.

This is a person who understands process and has experience with a sales cycle similar to yours. Also, you want sales people who are able to cut bait and move on. My experience has been that the most successful salespeople do not have the largest list of prospects, but a tight list of hunts.

Maxim: Do not hire new salespeople to sell outside of their old sales cycle experience.

Caution: A salesperson's expectations for success are developed in part around speed of result. When you hire people to sell in long sales cycles (say, 180 to 365 days) and their experience has been selling in shorter sales cycles (say, 30 to 90 days), the disconnect will lead to failure. The sales representative accustomed to faster and more wins will become discouraged and unproductive. The opposite is also true: a salesperson coming from a longer sales cycle experience into a shorter sales cycle business may lack the sense of urgency necessary to be successful. Hire people whose success has been in sync with the sales cycle of your business.

Give Them a Test

Before you make an offer, ask for a one-page business proposal in which the candidate explains how he or she would succeed at your company. Let the candidate set the deadline. This step will reveal the quality of five characteristics about the candidate:

- Ability to communicate in writing
- Understanding of the position
- Alignment with your company
- Ability to set goals and meet deadlines
- Ability to follow directions

Following these steps in hiring can help you maximize this market to find the dream candidates.

Hiring sales people is very challenging, but I believe that it will become easier rather than harder. The skills needed for sales success today are much more process-driven than charisma-driven. Process is easier to teach, measure, and coach to improve. Charisma is a quality that is hard to develop. In addition, as the world of selling moves from being relationship focused to relationships (plural) focused, the ability to be a good facilitator becomes important—and that, too, is a quality that can be developed.

Chapter 10: Coaching for Sales Performance

I'd like to share a time investment belief that I subscribe to when it comes to figuring out how to use your time with your salespeople. If you analyze your sales team, you may find that the ratio of 20:60:20 applies: 20 percent of your team members are very good, 60 percent are average, and 20 percent are on their way out. If you pull new hires from the ratio, it becomes even more accurate. The top 20 percent need support inside the organization and deal coaching on the larger opportunities in the field. The middle 60 percent need some development and more supervisory assistance. The bottom 20 percent, if they have been with your firm for a year or more, need to be moved out—and that takes time in most organizations because of policy compliance requirements.

So, what should your time investment be? Should it follow the same 20:60:20 ratio as your sales team's performance? NO! I believe it should look more like 50:30:20. That means that your time coaching is spent in strategy with the top performers and in skills application development in the middle group. Here's how a mentor of mine succinctly summarized it: "Feed your eagles and starve your turkeys."

The Three M's of Sales Leaders: Management, Magic, and Motivation

The three M's of sales leaders may seem obvious, but they can all too easily get thrown to the wayside in the course of a busy day, week, or month. If you follow a rigorous management process, you will have a productive and efficient sales team who you can then teach your magic, which will result in larger and more deals being landed. Once you have a team of salespeople who are following a process and working their own magic on prospects, if you can continuously motivate them through monetary and competitive incentives, then you have a recipe for long-term success. This is the goal of every sales leader.

#1: Management
Success in sales is 90 percent process and 10 percent magic.

Sales management is about process. Process, when done correctly, is boring. Isn't it? That's why so few managers do it—they want to perform the magic and forget the need for rigor. But the 90 percent of the time that a sales manager spends on process creates the opportunity for him or her to be magical during the 10 percent of time when sales leadership is necessary. In fact, the real leverage of magic comes because you have a process.

How to Manage Salespeople

Management and leadership in the world of sales are not the same thing. They have different goals, require different skills, and exercise different muscles. In my view, sales management focuses on the execution of a process. Think of it like manufacturing. There is a design and engineering phase, and then there is a production phase. The production phase is about efficiency and quality control. Sales management is what happens in the production phase of sales. To successfully manage salespeople during this production phase, I recommend the following:

1. Drive to a step process.

Just like manufacturing, for your sales production phase, you can set up a series of linked processes. In each process there are requirements to be completed before you can go to the next step. Sales management's role is to ensure that the process is being followed and that the execution is efficient and meets quality standards.

2. Only focus on the gaps.

It is tempting to try to armchair quarterback every deal in a weekly meeting with salespeople. Don't. The sales management process should point out gaps in either the information that is supposed to be gathered in a particular step of the sales process, a gap in the people who should be engaged, or a gap in how long that step is taking in comparison to your expectations. Focus on just those gaps. If there are no gaps, then the process is working. Focus on only those accounts with gaps.

3. Remember that compliance and coaching are different.

Coaching to solve gaps is a different exercise than ensuring that the machine is working. If you are brainstorming a solution for handling a thorny prospect or a stuck deal, set a separate meeting time. Production discussions are about running the machine, period.

4. Own the time.

Have your salespeople bring their calendars to their weekly meeting with you. Their calendar is not their own, it is yours. Working through the next week's or month's schedule is part of the meeting. These are the questions that sales management must ask as a part of the regular meetings: Where will we be next period? Are we going in the right direction with the right expectations? Are we visiting prospects or accounts just to visit or are we advancing the step-wise sales process?

How to Run the Sales Management Machine

I have seen as much as a 40 percent lift in productivity of sales people over a less than 90-day window in the companies that have implemented the following set of practices:

1. No group meetings.

Sale managers harbor a delusion that sales reps learn from each other as they discuss accounts at a sales meeting. The only person learning in a session like that is the salesperson who owns the account. In addition, that salesperson is usually evasive or defensive when put on the grill in front of his or her counterparts. Group meetings are for product and process education, recognition, and market planning—that's it.

2. Have weekly 1:1 meetings.

As a sales manager, you must drive sales process compliance and efficiency rep by rep and account by account. I advocate a 30-minute meeting every week with each rep for which you are responsible. Set it for the same time every week and run it the same way. I know, it's not sexy, but it is enormously effective.

3. Follow the thirty minute rule.

I jokingly say that all sales reps have ADHD unless they are the one talking, but the point is - don't have long meetings. A simple rule is thirty minutes of prep for you, per rep meeting, and thirty minutes of meeting with each of them, done every week. If you have five reps, that's five hours per week to run the machine. If you run the machine, the machine will run and run better. So what if it's boring. Remember: run the machine the right way and you get to make more magic.

4. Get commitments, take notes.

By running these 1:1 meetings every week, you should be able to instill rigor and impeccable follow-up in your salespeople, which is what is necessary for a good sales process. Take notes on what is to be done each week by each salesperson and start the next week's meeting with a status update on the prior week's commitments. Sounds simple, right? But lack of consistent rigor in holding people to their commitments is one of the biggest sales management mistakes I see.

5. Be Consistent

If you want to train others to think like you, ask them the same questions every time and they will soon anticipate your questions by beginning to ask those questions of themselves every time. Soon you will have people who think like you. If you play "gotcha" by asking all sorts of different questions, they will give up because they can't get it right. By working consistently according to a process, you can develop a series of management questions. By asking those consistently, you will soon get a group of salespeople who are following a consistent process. That's an efficient machine.

Now comes the fun part: when the machine is working as it should, you've got more time and energy for your magic. You've earned the right to do your magic by following your process.

#2: Magic
We call it "deal coaching," but trust me, it's magic.

This part of the job requires all the creativity, risk-taking, strategy, experience, and play-maker talent that I have, and I love it. I'm not alone—most of the sales leaders I know, regardless of title, love this part of the job the most.

There are three categories of sales leader magic:

1. Strategy: The big pieces here are market, product, big account sales, budget, and key account management. These are all areas where experience, insight, and instincts come together and can be brought to bear.

2. Coaching: This entails shaping the "how" and the "what" of the strategy. It manifests as tactics: helping your team know which tactic to use, when.

3. Troubleshooting: This involves the ability to decide what to do when you are out of tricks and have to conjure answers from thin air.

They all require a deep understanding of people—of what is possible with your own company and your prospect's company. You also bring your own broad background of hundreds of sales experiences, of winning and losing, to this effort to frame the right ideas and answers.

Guidelines for Great Sales Leader Magicians

1. Remember that battles are won before they're begun.

The best sales leader magicians do their work in the planning phase of each step in a managed process. This means that the important sales calls and meetings are roadmapped and role-played well in advance. It means that reactions, challenges, and objections are anticipated and considered and a protocol has been established for handling them before the meeting even takes place. Great strategy, like great magic, isn't done on the fly—and even though it's methodical, it is no less magic.

2. Let others shine.

I have worked with many sales leaders who have only one trick in their bag: "Take Me." They consider themselves the magic, which means that they see themselves as the only solution to challenges. Many times they are right: if they take center stage, they'll be amazing and the prospect will close. However, this tactic develops nothing and no one in the organization, and the role of the sales leader is to develop the magic in others, not just use his or her own skills to close. The best sales leaders, like the best coaches, stay on the sidelines most of the time.

For one sales leader I worked with, we set up a simple set of rules:

- If an opportunity was less than $100,000 in revenue, he could only provide insight when asked. He could not talk to the client by phone or participate in meetings.

- If an opportunity was between $100,000 and $250,000 in revenue, he could participate in client calls by phone, but not in sales calls.

- If an opportunity was more than $250,000 in revenue, he could participate in meetings.

The point of this example is not prescriptive. It does, however, illustrate my point that if the organization's salespeople are going to develop and the company is going to grow, magic must be sparingly used.

3. Show your work.

After seeing a sales leader perform his or her magic, a sales rep will try to imitate the same trick at another time in another place. For this reason, you need to explain your magic—why you did what you did and why this was the right time to do it. By explaining the situational limitations of using the trick, you will teach sales reps how and when to perform the trick, not just imitate it.

4. Do the same trick twice.

Magicians will tell you to never do the same trick twice because it becomes easier to figure out with repetition. For precisely that reason, I say do the same trick twice or more so that your people figure out why you are selecting a particular strategy and see how you are troubleshooting according to a model. When your team learns from you and improves, it increases the quality of the situations in which you get to use your magic.

5. Cluster your best tricks.

When I work with sales teams to develop a strategy for handling a given problem, my first question is, "Who else has a client or prospect for whom this approach would be a good fit right now?" Through leveraging up my efforts by attaching the strategy to other salespeople's issues, we have more impact and greater long-term traction.

6. When to do magic.

You'll find out which accounts require magic during your weekly sales management meetings. It is my strong recommendation that you not try to perform magic in that meeting. Rather, schedule another time when you can bring the right people, information, and mindset to the discussion. If you try to do magic on the spot, it could produce less than magical results.

Sales management is about process, sales magic is about application.

#3: Motivation
In business, it's all about the money.

You can follow a management process and conjure magic for your salespeople with the best of them, but in order to consistently land deals, you must keep your team motivated—and in sales, that means money.

Two simple ingredients go into sales: time and people.

Consistently landing deals, especially large accounts, requires holding the attention of salespeople for a long time. The time-to-money ratio is not 1:1 for a salesperson. The fact is that when you double the time it takes to land a deal, you have to practically triple the money to keep salespeople engaged.

Sure, part of that triple is built into the incremental commission of a bigger deal—and that can be a lot, depending on the size of the deal. But your salespeople will probably also need an extra something to keep them on task rather than getting distracted by little shiny objects, like deals that are small and fast to close. If they're not seeing their efforts translate into money in a meaningful way (profit sharing, bonus or incentive), they'll also too be distracted by the not-so-shiny-objects of their everyday job.

How to Use Money to Motivate

1. Pay more for big sales—and spread it around.

The sales representative is not the only person involved in the hunt. The fact is, after the initial interest is generated, the internal subject matter expert (SME) team does a lot of the heavy lifting. If your SME team, creative people, and others involved in the process are all motivated to land the deal, your salespeople will feel that and will keep the momentum. Keep the whole team involved happy by giving a piece of the cake to all, no matter how small. The compensation model shifts from paying big commissions to salespeople to a more shared compensation and bonus model for growth.

This new model will require that compensation for the organization reflect the growth of the business, either through adding new accounts or growing current accounts. Everyone will need to hunt bigger—but the idea is that with proper coaching they will be able to, and with appropriate compensation they will want to.

2. Put a trophy-bonus on the wall.

Make it specific and personal. At one point in my career, I had a competitor for whom I had a personal distaste. I put a list of that competitor's top ten clients on the wall and told my team, "I will pay a 20 percent premium on commissions for every deal we land from this list in the next six months." We got three, and it tasted sweet. Not only did the money motivate my team, but the incentive of beating the competitor brought out their best work.

3. Cut out the money on little deals.

You can't get people focused on bigger targets if they get the same ratios of money for the smaller one-off deals. Cut little deal commissions in half. This is about changing behaviors and time investment.

Advice for Managing New Sales Representatives

Your coaching hours are a precious resource. You must guard them, leverage them with other systems of training and development that your company provides, and then invest them well. These are especially important guidelines to be aware of when coaching new salespeople. Here are some tips to get everyone off on the right foot:

- **Keep the representative on a short leash.** The rep at first will need you to set daily goals regarding contact activity and the data gathered, and eventually prospects and calls. This isn't micromanagement; it is just holding onto the bike while the kid gets used to riding without training wheels.

- **Take the first hits.** For the rep's first calls to prospects, make them conference calls with you on the line. Let the rep listen to you and help him or her gain confidence in this new space.

- **Keep your foot on the gas.** Shift from planning into action and keep up the intensity of your expectations.

Although it is emotionally rewarding to see babies take their first steps, your job as a sales leader is to get sales people productive quickly and then move them to excellence. If you are continuing to invest time and energy in a person who has not responded with lifts in performance in the past, you are the one at blame. They move up or they move on. Make your investments knowing that their performance is a far stronger reflection of what they do with what you give them than it is a reflection on you.

Part 3: Sales Maximization

Introduction

My father was a salesman. I rode along with him on sales calls from the age of twelve. I listened to him prospect on the phone to get appointments, heard him rehearse presentations, and then listened to him debrief me in the car after calls. Sometimes, if he was visiting a client he knew well, I would even get to sit in the meeting. I learned a lot. One core lesson was the pragmatic nature of salespeople. My dad and most salespeople want to know, "What do I have to do on my next call in order to win?"

In these chapters, I will address the most common issues that experienced and successful salespeople repeatedly tell me are the biggest challenges in selling. In a nutshell, they are:

- How to get access to the highest-level decision makers
- How to differentiate their company in a commoditized market
- How to unstick deals that are stuck

I have answers for you, but they're not simplistic, "when they say/do this, you say/do that" answers. Those are the verbal fencing skills and situational selling approaches of the dying world of selling. Some of those techniques still work, but let's be honest: you're already using most of them. The challenge we face today is that when the rules of buying changed the rules of selling, those skills became less effective.

My framework for answering these key challenges is based on a few anchoring beliefs:

1. You get sent to whom you sound like. To get an Executive Sponsor decision maker to engage in your selling process, you cannot message or motivate change the same way you have in the past. New buyers mean new messages.

2. The company with the most information wins. Buyers don't care how much you know or how much you care. That's old thinking. They want to know how much you can help them win in their marketplace and deal with their problems and their competitors. You must have different and better information than anyone else in order to meet that requirement.

3. It takes a team—on both sides. Decision power has moved away from the end user. The end user is still at the table; just not alone. You now have procurement, engineering, IT, marketing, and more at the table, too. They all need to be persuaded, or they can kill the deal, individually or together. Those specialists from the buying team do not want to hear a salesperson answering their questions. They want answers from their positional peers in your company. Selling is about directing a choir, not singing a solo.

4. If you get caught selling, you lose. Buyers are jaded. They have heard promises, seen PowerPoint presentations, and read proposals. Too often, buyers feel that they were promised one thing and received another. All of that makes their radar go off with loud sirens when they feel they are being sold. They don't want promises and reassurances. They want specifics about how you are going to solve their problems.

The chapters that follow are a mixture of techniques and templates for overcoming these big challenges in the new world of selling. It is possible that they will always be challenges, but my hope is that with these tools, you will be better than your competitors at winning.

Chapter 11: The Role of the Modern Sales Professional

What is a salesperson's role in this new business-to-business, buyer's economy? The changed model of selling and buying has forced salespeople to move upstream to a marketplace that focuses on complex, large sales opportunities. So, first and foremost, it is important to adapt your sales skills in order to be relevant to that marketplace. Sales professionals are no longer expected to be at the front of all product and service knowledge. Nor are they expected to be the sole conduit to customers of information about their organization. Their efforts are facilitated by marketing messages pushed out by corporate headquarters or through available information that can be accessed through the Internet. These developments leave a very different world and set of priorities for the sales professional.

How does this new world affect the buyer/seller relationship? Governance policies of buying organizations are decreasing buyers' ability to connect with salespeople and develop relationships in ways that were the norm until not too many years ago. No more going out to lunch or dinner, going to the ball game, or hunting and fishing trips. These have been excluded to the point where you can't even buy someone a cup of coffee as a part of the selling process for fear that this would violate a policy.

In addition, schedules have become so cluttered that it can be hard to get an extended meeting with a buyer for general information gathering and needs assessment. So much has been trimmed out to make the process of introducing a selling company to a buying company as efficient and impersonal as possible. As a result, all your time with a buyer is focused on task, with little to no time for trust- and relationship-building.

Does this mean that salespeople provide little or no value to the sales process in the new business-to-business economy? No. But what they bring to the table is significantly different from what they have brought to the table in the past. In the past, success was driven by hard work, forging lots of relationships, and having many prospects in the pipeline—the famous funnel principle that has held sway for decades, as discussed in Chapter 8. In the new marketplace, it is about doing less but being very, very effective about it. It means having a shorter list of prospects in your pipeline, but all of those prospects being highly qualified. And it means accepting your role as one of many players in a selling process developed by a large organization committed to hunting big game. **The future of sales relationship building will be about more people inside of fewer companies, not fewer people inside of more companies.**

These kinds of skills call for a different type of sales professional. For business-to-business sales professionals, going upstream to solve bigger problems for bigger organizations at higher levels means that you will be applying your innate skill set in a very different way.

The Process

In the past, relationship development was the highest value, followed by hard work. In the new economy, the most effective sales professionals will be masterful at project management and at facilitating the complex process of development of trust between two organizations with disparate cultures and the various personalities working within them. Big deals require lots of people, lots of details, and a defined process. Getting the people and the process right will define successful sales management in the future.

As I see it, the sales process in its broadest sense unfolds in three phases:

Phase 1: Secure an Executive Sponsor

As I will discuss in detail in Chapter 12, by having an Executive Sponsor, you secure the proper level of executive oversight and motivation for a successful execution of the buying process. It doesn't guarantee that you will win, but it does give you some degree of confidence that you will have the right people in the right room at the right time talking about the right problems. If you look at the curve of fear and the curve of advantage in the illustration, you'll notice that the curve of advantage is most highly represented in the securing of an Executive Sponsor. Executive Sponsors are looking for a solution to a large problem, so the best way to secure one is to convince him or her of the core advantage that will be delivered to the buying company by choosing you as a provider.

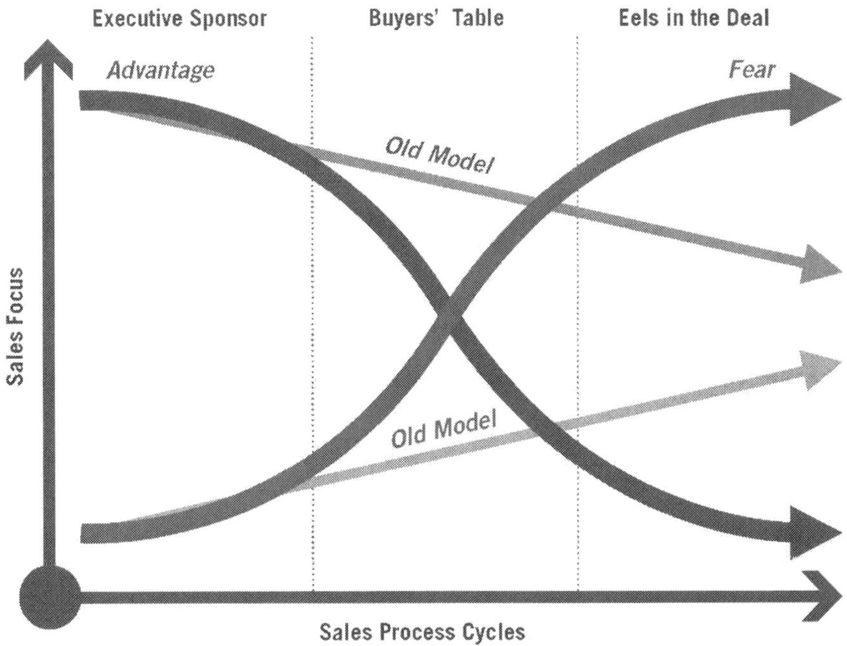

Phase 2: Get the Right People at the Table

The second phase comprises what happens at the table. You'll see in the illustration that there's a point where the curve of advantage and the curve of fear intersect. In Phase 2, advantage starts to drop off as the driving issue of the conversation, and fear picks up momentum. The reason is simple: The buyer's table members are going to have to live with their choices. Their fears show up in the form of questions about how things will work, what the success rate has been in the past, what milestones will demonstrate success, and whether there are off-ramps on this highway to hell. They consider it to be a highway to hell because change—even positive change—represents more work and more risk for them, and until they see a clear way to heaven, they fear they're going to hell.

Suppose you're not getting the buy-in you need because you don't have the right people at the table. We recommend five core strategies.

1. Appeal to the bigger problem. One of the best ways to get organizations to commit resources to the table is to make certain that they see the problem as being big and urgent enough to become an "A-List" priority. It is your responsibility as the selling organization to frame the impact of the problem by showing the buyer organization the pain that would result from not taking action now. If the answer is, "We can always do this later," chances are that the real answer is, "We will always do this later." Postponing a choice, decision, or commitment of resources is easier than saying an outright no.

2. Make the problem and its solution relevant to the person or department. Suppose you're in IT, finance, operations, or some other department, and a solution is brought to the table that does not directly affect you and your department. It is likely that you will try to avoid the meetings, not review the materials, and only participate minimally in the process. As a salesperson, you can expect to encounter this type of behavior during the selling process. One of your responsibilities is to ensure that everyone on both sides of the table understands how participating in the buying process is relevant to their particular job and work.

3. Increase traction with insights into the market. The fact is that sometimes the issue is not relevant to a given individual or department, but you still need that individual's or department's involvement. For example, IT is one of those departments that touches everything, although not everything is relevant to IT. Given that IT is generally already grappling with a long list of work orders and a busy calendar, it is easy to see why IT may balk at participating in a new solution or opportunity.

One way to get people to participate in the meetings and conversations is to offer insights and unique information in your meetings that they might not otherwise gain. It may be research, best practices, evaluation, case studies, or other things that are forward-looking. When your meetings provide executives with insights that will make them more effective, you may be surprised at the increased attendance.

4. Create a more dynamic meeting agenda. Most agendas are simply lists of topics to be discussed. A list is not particularly compelling and can lead some to think that they can skip class and get the notes from someone else who attended. But if you develop your meeting agenda by asking, "What are the outcomes that will happen from this particular meeting?" and create the agenda from there, you increase the likelihood that higher-level executives will attend. Why? Because now you can contact your Executive Sponsor and say, "Here's the agenda for the meeting. Here's what we're looking to accomplish. Can we accomplish this with the people who have been invited and in the amount of time we've been given?"

That question can bring people to the table and add productive time to the process. That agenda will focus the meeting dynamically on choices and decisions to be made, rather than on topics to be reviewed. For more information on how to create a dynamic agenda, see Chapter 16.

I'm always surprised by the number of meetings that I attend in which there is no clear set of outcomes designated to happen at the end of a meeting. **The only reason to meet is to make choices and decisions.** If it's just about information transfer, that can happen by digital means. **We bring people together to come to conclusions.**

5. Never call it selling. To bring people in your own organization to the table, including your most important subject matter experts, focus on the idea that the purpose of each and every meeting is to solve a problem, not to sell a good or service. Obviously, I personally am a fan of selling, but I'm realistic enough to know getting engineers to attend a sales call is not as easy as getting engineers to attend a problem-solving meeting. Their minds, skills, and training are aimed at solving problems. When you ask them to attend a session to help solve a problem, their excitement and energy rise. When you ask them to attend a sales call, they look for the door and claim that they've got a dental appointment.

Phase 3: Deal with the Eels

In the third phase, you deal with the eels. We describe eels as anyone who is actively or passively against making the commitment to a significant opportunity at this moment. Eels are not always openly hostile to your organization or solution. In fact, some of the most dangerous eels are those who are in favor of doing what you are suggesting, but they want to do it more slowly and they want to do less of it right now so that they can "test things out."

Remember that fear curve we looked at earlier? Eels have the highest level of fear. Because they are the most fearful, they must be identified early and reassured often with ways to mitigate their fears, including what implementation will look like, as change represents work and risk to them.

Ultimately in this new world of selling, it is fear—including yours—that will dictate the speed and scale of a sale. If you are fearful, you will take smaller steps, and you will take them more slowly. The same goes for everyone on both sides of the table, even when the advantage of making the change is clear. The better you are at addressing the various players' fears, the faster things will move and the larger the decision will be.

The Five Highest-Value Actions

Of all the things that you do as a sales professional, there are five actions that will bring the highest yield and are most valued by your buying organizations. We'll be talking about them in the chapters that follow. They include:

1. Securing Executive Sponsorship from your prospect company
2. Assembling a Buyer's Table of high-level influencers in the decision-making process
3. Performing reconnaissance for needs, audits, market relevance, and other materials
4. Process management of both the buying and selling process for both companies

5. Facilitation of trust development and negotiated custom solutions between the two companies

Perhaps you can see from this discussion that with the market shift in the buyer's power, the role of the sales professional has been elevated. This is a good thing. The sales professional now is a leader of a team of executives selling to a team of executives. This means bigger opportunities to solve bigger problems. For the sales professional, it provides the stage for using broader skills and having a more significant impact on the buying and selling company alike.

Chapter 12: Securing the Executive Sponsor

Typically, the success rate for "blind" inquiries in the marketplace is less than 3 to 5 percent. "Blind" means that the seller has not secured an Executive Sponsor, has no prior working history with the buying company, and does not have a clear understanding of the problem before receiving the inquiry.

In Chapter 9, I briefly defined and outlined the capabilities of an Executive Sponsor. We're going to take a deeper dive now. An Executive Sponsor is someone in your prospect company who:

1. Has the authority to make a purchasing decision. Although large opportunities commonly require multiple approvals and signatures, an Executive Sponsor has the authority to sign the contract as one of the key executives making the decision to approve the purchase and release funds.

2. Has the power to convene. An Executive Sponsor has the ability to pull together the necessary people to participate in a sales process, information-gathering process, and finally, recommendation process to come to a purchasing decision.

3. Has the problem you can solve. An Executive Sponsor sees the problem you can solve as a priority that he or she wants to get fixed. All executives are focusing on their "A-list" priorities. So, you have to make certain that the problem that you are solving is on that executive's A-list. That doesn't mean that someone might not be a valuable supporter of an issue that's not on his or her A-list. It just means that he or she doesn't qualify to be your Executive Sponsor.

In addition, your Executive Sponsor must agree to do the following five things on your behalf. If this person isn't willing to do these five things, it means either that you and your organization are not viewed as bringing a potential resolution to the problem that this person is trying to solve, or that this person is not convinced that it's worth spending the necessary time and energy to see a successful completion of the process. (Note that when I say "a successful completion of the process", I mean that the outcome may include the Executive Sponsor not selecting you, or the company not selecting you, as the provider of products or services.)

Here are the five things that an Executive Sponsor must be willing to provide:

1. **Access.** An Executive Sponsor must be willing to assist you in connecting your organization with the right people in his or her organization.
2. **Priority.** An Executive Sponsor must be willing to declare that this is an important priority and to give you and your organization appropriate amounts of response time and attention for you to do your work.
3. **Interest.** An Executive Sponsor needs to demonstrate interest in what is going on by staying in the loop. This simply means responding to your e-mails and voicemails and taking steps to keep up to date with what is going on in the process of evaluating whether your organizations may work together.
4. **Clarity.** It is very likely that along the way you will come up against things that you do not understand. There may be obstacles, political situations, snafus, and snares. Your Executive Sponsor must be willing to provide some clarity so that you do the right thing and best represent your organization's ability to help move through this particular process.
5. **Authority and ability to clear logjams.** If the process slows down for some reason, you need your Executive Sponsor to assist in pushing through the obstacles that are impeding progress of the sales process.

You'll notice that you aren't asking Executive Sponsors to do anything illegal, immoral, or unethical. You haven't asked this person to favor you, demonstrate some sort of preference that you be the selected vendor or partner, or confer any unfair advantage. You have simply asked the Executive Sponsor to provide the necessary resources and commitment for you to perform an effective evaluation of the buying organization's needs and to design your potential solution.

Think of it this way: every step in a sales process costs your organization thousands in actual dollars as well as in opportunity cost. You want to make certain that you have an Executive Sponsor before you start to spend that money. You ask for these five items to ensure that you are willing to invest your company's time and energy in the sales process and because you believe that in the end, as a result of this process, enough resources will have been committed by the buying organization to help both parties determine whether or not you are the right provider.

If someone does not provide Executive Sponsorship, the likelihood that you will win the sales process is very, very low. The drag of inertia is so great that the buyer organization will likely default to the status quo, whether that means sticking with the current and incumbent provider, or simply doing nothing at all. It requires true Executive Sponsorship to get change to happen, so you had better make certain that you have Executive Sponsorship before you do anything else. That is a prime duty of the sales professional in the modern business-to-business economy.

I have included an example of what an Executive Sponsorship agreement might look like. Many of the companies we work with use a version of this agreement and put it in front of their prospective Executive Sponsor during the sales process.

Now, I want to be very clear: I would never ask an Executive Sponsor to sign this type of document. People are very, very concerned about liability, contract management, and governance. Asking someone to sign something is presumptuous and inappropriate in the sales process until we get to the point of a purchase order, statement of work, or contract. What we are asking is to set clear expectations between us and the buyer as to what works best as far as expenditure of resources on both sides of the table. By getting their commitment up front, we know that they take us seriously, and we can then expend resources and take them seriously.

When do you use this document? Well, once you have identified the key decision maker in the process and have secured his or her interest, you ask for Executive Sponsorship. It is absolutely paramount that you be clear that you are not asking for the favoritisms I've described earlier. What you are doing at that particular moment is conducting a litmus test to determine if this individual is willing and able to commit to the process of your companies' evaluating each other for potential future work.

What if the person says no? You should expect that, on occasion, this will happen. You may get a no because you misread the situation and thought you had the support you needed when in fact the person was not yet ready to be that supportive. You may get a no because the person is concerned about the risk of violating a governance requirement or about having implied favoritism in some way despite your clear reassurances to the contrary. You may find that people say no because they're simply not ready. All three of these answers and others are still good signs—because they tell you what you should do next.

What you should do at this point is to take responsibility for the possibility that you've either not explained the value of what you bring to the table that would merit their Executive Sponsorship, or that you have not explained why Executive Sponsorship is necessary for your company to invest in the process at all. A "no" gives you the chance to explain these two points and then retest the waters.

If you still receive a negative response, then you have to explain to the potential Executive Sponsor that your organization can't write blank checks into the process without knowing that it has a sincere and interested partner on the other side. What you don't want to do is get trapped into a pricing exercise or into a market scan on the part of the buying company. Remember, it costs them nothing to make you jump through all sorts of hoops in the overall buying process and to thereby garner all sorts of market information and intelligence.

Only when they are willing to commit their time resources do you know that you actually have parity in the conversation and the potential for coming out with a contract. In my research for my book RFP's Suck, I learned that statistically, 88 percent of all buying processes result with the renegotiation or a re-up of the contract with the incumbent. That's right,

88 percent. The only way to drop that number in your favor is to make certain that you have Executive Sponsorship before you move forward.

For years, I have used this technique of securing an Executive Sponsor early in a sales process as a way to gauge true interest as well as to set expectations for a buyer in a large and complex sale. There have been occasions when I have asked more than one person in a prospect company to serve this role. However, it wasn't until the past few years that I have had clients write down what Executive Sponsorship means in a one-page document and give it to the candidate in a meeting. While the verbal-only approach was effective, the use of the one-page letter has been amazing.

Take a look at the sample letter below and see if it works for you. It should be printed on your letterhead, with the title "Executive Sponsorship" at the top:

(Your Company Letterhead)

Executive Sponsorship

Dear Key Decision Maker,

We know that moving forward with a partner requires the work of a number of people. We also know that without senior executive sponsorship, the work of the day and competing priorities keeps organizations from moving initiatives like this along. We are not asking you to agree to do business with us at this point. It's too early. We are asking for you to be our Executive Sponsor through the process. For us this simply means:

Access. Your assistance in connecting to the right people is very important.

Priority. We will look to you to set the appropriate level of attention for your organization so that the process is supported.

Interest. We will be communicating with you throughout the process about what is happening. Let's stay connected back and forth on the progress.

Logjams. If the process bogs down, we need to be able to come to you and to count on your assistance.

Clarity. There are times when we will need to better understand your company and its unique culture. If we are confused, we ask you to provide clarity.

I'll close this chapter with a story from my own consulting experience. I was speaking with the president of one of my client companies. He was a very aggressive, very dynamic sales professional, but when I introduced the idea of an Executive Sponsorship agreement, I could see him visibly pale. He was nervous about what would happen in the sales process when he put this litmus test in front of his prospect. But like all good leaders, he was willing to lead from the front. The next time we spoke, he was full of pride because he had done exactly what we had talked about: putting the agreement in front of someone and making certain that this person was willing to be his Executive Sponsor. When I asked him what happened, he said, "I kind of hemmed and hawed through the very end of the process, before I put that Executive Sponsorship in front of him, and I was a little bit nervous. I've sold lots of deals over the course of time, but I still could feel my hand shaking a little bit when I put that piece of paper on the table and slid it across to the buyer. I know I said something about the idea that we like to set out expectations of how we might work together, and that we put this together for his review. He took a moment and read through the document from top to bottom. Then he set down the piece of paper and looked at me and he said, 'You guys have got your act together. I'll be your Executive Sponsor.'"

It's not easy to ask for this level of Executive Sponsorship support, but in the new business-to-business world, where so much expense and effort can be poured into processes that often do not yield new relationships, it is critical to know early where you stand with your Executive Sponsor. Each step along the way in the sales process, as you add more executives and more subject matter experts, it will be appropriate for you to consider whether or not to secure additional Executive Sponsorship using an agreement in those conversations. And on each occasion when you are dealing with someone who will be involved in signing off, in signing the contract, in authorizing the utilization of a portion of his or her budget, or in reviewing final terms and conditions, it is wise to consider securing that individual's Executive Sponsorship.

Remember, this is about gaining clarity on what it will take to make certain that both parties are wisely investing their time and energy in a process that will yield a good outcome for both companies. One potential outcome is that your company decides that it doesn't want the work. Another is that they decide that you're not the right partner. And then, of course, there is the third potential outcome, which is that you secure a new relationship and a new contract.

Statistically, in the more than 700 companies we have worked with, most have tracked and told us that the use of this single document more than doubles the conversion rate. I've been in this world of large account sales for more than thirty years and am viewed as one of the foremost experts, and I, too, find that this simple tool has a disproportionate yield. By simply using this in your process, you will get more from your overall sales efforts than from almost any other single tool, technique, or tip that I can provide.

Chapter 13: Assembling a Buyer's Table of High-Level Influencers

If you're going to be effective in the world of large account selling in the current and near-future economy, then you have to become comfortable with larger numbers—not just the larger economic scale of the deal, but also the larger number of people involved. There are a lot of reasons why large sales mean large tables. We'll explore some of the key reasons below.

Complexity

We like to joke that in the modern business culture, you cannot pave a parking lot without the involvement of someone from the IT department. One of the reasons why large sales require so many people is because ERP systems, SCM systems, CRM systems, and all sorts of variations of these organization-wide, integrated data management systems have made the simplest things complex.

There are reasons for this. As organizations have implemented concepts like just-in-time inventory, Six Sigma manufacturing principles, lean manufacturing, and the Theory of Constraints, they have had to develop methods for meeting their commitment to continuous process improvement. Automated systems make it possible for organizations to view dashboards showing almost real-time activity for key data points that make a system flow more efficiently and effectively.

No matter what product, service, or ongoing solution you're bringing in, it will have a ripple effect at various touch points throughout your customer's complex network of processes, and there will have to be points of input everywhere throughout the system. For this reason, all of the touch points must have representation at the buyer's table to ensure that their activities will not be interrupted by your great solution.

The more people who are added to the table, the more likely it is that there will be resistance inside the organization to almost any new idea, because it may be viewed as an interruption (or worse, as a threat) to their current work and accustomed methods of operation.

Consensus

There's always concern about alignment of priorities. Organizations live within a resource constraint: An infinite number of demands are being applied against a finite amount of resources, and each employee has his or her own set of priorities. Only by aligning all of the contributing parties' priorities will it be possible for an organization to devote the necessary people, time, and additional resources to the successful implementation of a new product, service, or solution. If you do not bring all of the representative parties to the table for the conversation, somewhere in the selling process, they will bite you in the backside later in the process by saying that they are resource-constrained and that this is not a number-one priority for their particular area, department or division.

Of course, the idea of cultural buy-in has become pervasive in organizational lore over the past three decades. Consensus-driven organizations seek a level of commitment from all members participating in change so that they can be assured of more complete implementation throughout the organization. Although this sounds ideal in theory, it can be enormously frustrating in its execution. Consensus-driven organizations have a tendency to shape their final solution to the **lowest common dominator,** adopting the least offensive change that everyone can tolerate, rather than selecting the highest-performing level of change for the organization's long-term goals. But whatever is ultimately decided, the fact is that you're going to have bigger tables because more people will need to buy in.

Integration

As I've mentioned, technologies—enterprise resource planning, customer relationship management, invoicing systems, and online systems, to name just a few—provide vital data about performance and integrate the many moving parts of organizations. I've never encountered an organization that has said, in effect: "We love having new projects because our technology resources are a little underutilized." It just doesn't happen. In fact, IT departments always believe themselves to be under-resourced and overextended. Put all of these factors together and you have the reason why any change requires a technology involvement and presence at the table.

Oversight

I've discussed elsewhere in this book how the advent of greater degrees of compliance and governance has dictated higher levels of oversight and involvement by a wide variety of people to ensure that all of the organization's procedures and protocols are followed. Some of this has to do with regulation; some with financial protocols; some is simply what happens when dealing with bureaucracy. Regardless of the driver, governance creates a need to increase the number of people at the table during a significant purchase so that all of the details can be checked off as being compliant.

Motivations for Buyers to Control Table Size

So here we are, with all of these people at the table—despite the stated desire of buying and selling organization alike to increase efficiency by using fewer resources in every process! If this sounds counterintuitive, that's because it is. There are in fact a number of motivations on the buyer's side of the equation to decrease the number of people participating in the decision, and there are ways you can work with those motivations to ensure that you've got the right people at the table.

Buyer Motivator #1: Influencing the Buyer

There is a fear of your organization, the seller, influencing the buyer. That's right. The buying organization is afraid that you will be effective in persuading end users and other members of the organization to sign off on a decision that is not necessarily financially in the best interest of the buying organization. This lack of trust is unfortunate, but it is real. Because buying organizations are afraid of your effectiveness, they try to make all interactions in the buying process as antiseptic and as objective as possible. This is why you see so much reliance on purchasing and procurement departments, instead of simple specification and negotiation at the end user level. Once specs have been defined, it is typical for the organization to hand off vendor selection to purchasing or procurement with the belief that the folks in those departments have the skills to negotiate a better price, terms, and conditions, than those that can be negotiated by the overly enthusiastic (so they fear) end user buyer.

Buyer Motivator #2: Conflict of Interest

There are always concerns about conflict of interest. In the last twenty years, the behaviors of some bad actors in the selling process have become examples of the need for transparency and a more objective approach to securing products and services. We all know about the $500 toilet seat in the Pentagon or the $250 hammer that was purchased as a part of some public investigation of misused funds. The hard lessons of these incidents have been codified in regulation and law, to the degree that organizations are deathly afraid that there will be an appearance of impropriety in their purchasing.

To insulate themselves from charges of impropriety, as well as to make certain that later on, if challenged by shareholders or by other participants in the selling process, organizations have tried to turn all sales processes into a comparative evaluation between qualified selling companies, rather than a presentation and persuasion of the value of one company versus another. Put another way, they would like all buying activities to occur in a vacuum without the presence and influence of highly trained and effective salespeople. Thus we find ourselves selling into organizations that are trying to diminish the number and levels of people in their company who participate in the final purchasing decision—in direct opposition to what we know as most important, which is increasing the number of buying participants in the sales process to ensure that we have a complete understanding of the problem being resolved and that we have specifications that will meet the end user's final desires.

Buyer Motivator #3: Feature-Driven Final Decision

The unfortunate truth about procurement and purchasing as departments is that they are motivated and even incented to get the lowest possible cost for the minimum standard of performance. Procurement and purchasing are supposed to determine the absolute lowest standard necessary to meet the requirements of the end user and to not to pay for or allow for the presence of one additional feature beyond that stated specification. End users, in contrast, are tasked with defining exactly what the product, service, or solution is supposed to provide and then allowing procurement and purchasing to negotiate price for that defined product or service. Allowing end users into the buying decision means that the decision-making process will be feature-driven, rather than price or cost-driven.

By allowing more end users into the process, organizations are taking the risk that features considered by some to be "nice to have" will be mandated as "must-have" in the final specification for purchase. They combat this by decreasing the number of participants in the buying process to ensure that they get the leanest definition of specification, thereby decreasing the price of the final choice.

Buyer Motivator #4: Time

The last several decades have seen the elimination of all sorts of levels of support inside organizations. Anyone who has been in business for more than two decades remembers a time when they had more time to do their work, consider alternatives and solutions, keep up with what's going on in the industry, make contacts, and so on. These days, middle levels of management and support staff have been removed or dramatically reduced. Everyone has more and bigger decisions to make, but less and less time in which to make them.

Organizations therefore want to keep their people focused on the task at hand and spending less time discussing pros and cons with outside salespeople. Internal and external policies have been put in place that keep employees at their desks, in their cubicles, and with their nose to the grindstone. This is one more reason why your prospect will naturally be resistant to adding people to the sales process, even in instances when it would make the discussion more efficient and accelerate the process.

Motivations for Sellers to Control Table Size

Sellers, for their part, also have reasons for trying to decrease the number of participants in the sales process. Unfortunate as this is, **salespeople often say that the toughest sale they have to make is internally—within their own company.** There are a number of reasons why this occurs, but I will only cover four of them.

Seller Motivator #1: Lack of Understanding

Often, sellers do not understand that there has been a shift in the buying behaviors of organizations. It's interesting to listen to senior executives talk nostalgically about the longstanding personal relationships they built with big buyers and big companies back in the days when they were selling—which could be two to three decades ago. "Why do we need all of these meetings with all of these people?" they ask. Because they haven't been out in the field in recent years, they haven't experienced and therefore don't fully realize how the buying world has changed. As a result, senior executives in the selling organization may be reluctant to allow other team members to accompany sales reps to meetings or even attend the meetings themselves, or to allocate resources to a deal that they believe could be done by the rep alone via one-on-one meetings with the prospect. This is how reps find themselves "selling" the idea of team and executive participation to their own people.

Seller Motivator #2: Everyone Is Pressed for Time

It's not just the buying organizations that feel the constraints of limited resources and the lack of available staff and time. Selling organizations feel the same pinch. Subject matter experts were in high demand even before their presence at the table became important in the selling process. They guard their time, as most busy, productive people in lean organizations must do today. Resource and time constraints are driving much of group face time out of the sales process, just when it is needed the most.

Seller Motivator #3: Lack of Confidence in the Opportunity

If senior management believes that the sales opportunity is real and that there is a high likelihood of landing it, their willingness to allow their subject matter experts, key executives, and others to attend sales presentation meetings will rise dramatically. Everyone wants to be a part of landing a new piece of business. But if senior management has little sense of which deal is more likely to land than another, they look at all of them with the same skeptical eye and say, in effect, "This deal probably won't land, and it's a bad use of our peoples' time."

On a related note, key subject matter experts often resist participating in presenting because they're afraid of selling, or they hang onto the cliché that selling is in some ways a dirty business populated by used car sales types, and that it's about glad-handing, entertaining, charming, and persuading. When subject matter experts understand that there is no such thing as "selling" in a large account, but rather that there is a need for **solving** in a large account, their willingness to attend goes up, as they see their role as being an expert who helps to solve a problem rather than sell a deal.

Buyer's Bait: How to Get the Right Decision Makers to the Table

In most key account sales, the size of the deal and the number of people involved in the decision is directly proportional. The challenge is getting all of the necessary people involved in the process. Without the right people in the conversation, you are either delayed, delegated, or dead. You need "bait" to bring the right people to the conversation. Here are four ways to do that:

1. People: You need to leverage the most senior executive in your prospect to bring others to the table.

2. Information: Offer insights they want by enticing key players with an Executive Briefing you have prepared about changes in the prospect's industry, market, regulation, or technology. Being "them-centric" rather than focused on your own issues builds goodwill and trust.

3. Time: Break up a long meeting into fifteen- to thirty-minute increments so that

participants see their investment as being smaller than a two-hour session of which only a small portion will be of direct interest to them.

4. Insight: Offer to present an assessment or analysis of a component of the business that will show where the prospect stands as compared to the industry.

In each of these cases, the focus is on the people you are attracting, not you, your product, or what you offer. That focus on the buyer's interests and needs increases the likelihood of attendance.

So, What About You?

What is the role of the modern sales representative? Your job is to get the right people on both sides of the equation to the table, communicating about the right things, in the right order, to solve the right problem. The more successful you are at doing that, the greater the likelihood that big decisions can be made with the full support of the buying organization and full commitment to execution from the selling organization. That's how everyone wins.

Chapter 14: Getting Reconnaissance Right

Salespeople often concentrate on explaining to prospects all the virtues of the products or services they offer. That works just fine . . . for small sales. But if you want to move into the world of big deals, you have to change your approach. You'll still talk about your product or service, but you'll focus on your prospects' problems, approach, and process. Of course, you have to know what those are. That's why the key to your success in landing big deals lies in quality of the information you get.

You can learn many facts about your prospect from the prospect's website, annual report, strategic plan, or RFP. But so can your competitors. What you want is deeper information, not just facts. You want information that isn't readily available to the public or to other people within the company or the current incumbent. You want information that will help you match your prospects' problems to your solutions. You want information your competitors don't have.

How do you get this information? You ask questions. But the traditional questions you have learned to ask aren't sufficient. They might be good questions, but they could be great questions. Good questions are often general and vague, which means that the answers you get will be the same. I have used this device of turning good questions into great questions with my clients for a number of years. The questions have gained quite a bit of traction for them in their hunts for big deals.

The Qualities of Great Questions

First, let's look at how great questions differ from good ones.

- **They're specific.** Great questions drive to the heart of the issue. When you frame your questions in the ways I'm about to suggest, you'll get measurable answers that pertain directly to what you need to know.
- **They're historical.** Past behavior is the best indicator of future behavior. Asking about specific circumstances from the past gives you a unique vision of how your prospect operates.

- **They're narrative.** When you hear a prospect say, "I remember this one time that we . . . ," you know that you're about to hear a story. In telling the story, the prospect will give you context and emotion in addition to information. Emotional connection is key to active selection rather than just sleep-walking to the default of doing what that person has always done.
- **They're behavioral.** We want to know what people have done or will do, not just what their opinions are. Great questions elicit that information.
- **They make people vulnerable.** You want to learn about the authentic person in the conversation. Great questions allow you to learn who the real buyer is, who is most affected by your solution, and who can do you the most harm, among other things.
- **They help you gauge a prospect's interest.** You get clues from great Q&A sessions that are hard to find any other way. For example, if a buyer gives you general answers to your specific questions, he or she is probably not interested in doing the deal with you. Buyers who are completely evasive or say they don't have time to answer definitely aren't interested. Buyers who take the time to consider what you've asked and to give you a complete answer are more likely to be interested in working with you.

By crafting questions with these types of characteristics, you are opening the possibility of accessing a level of knowledge that is deeper, more indicative, and more valuable than what your competitors may be able to get. For example, when you are in the qualification stage, you want to know if this is a great opportunity for you or if you should disqualify the prospect. To make that decision, you need the following kinds of information: Is this a real opportunity or a waste of time? Who is the real decision maker? Can we win if we are not the lowest priced? Am I talking to the right people? What will it take to win this business through my proposal?

These are reasonable and straightforward questions, but you won't get reasonable and straightforward responses from your prospects by asking them. The conversation is likely to go like this:

Q: "Is this a real opportunity or a waste of time?"

A: "It's a real opportunity."

Q: "Can we win if we are not the lowest priced?"

A: "Of course."

Q: "Am I talking to the right people?"

A: "Yes—me."

Q: "What will it take to win this business through my proposal?

A: "Hard work."

You'll learn nothing of value from these answers. To get great value, you need to ask great questions.

Here are some useful general rules about asking questions that also apply to asking great questions:

- Never be accusatory or personal.
- Keep your questions short and to the point.
- Address only one topic per question.
- Listen carefully to the answer. Don't concentrate on the next question you want to ask.
- Don't ask questions that can be answered with a single word.

CATAPULT Your Way to Great Questions

In order to help my clients become more effective at getting information, I provide a way to remind them of key elements for great question construction. It's an acronym that spells the word CATAPULT, and each letter represents a specific kind of great question:

C=Change

A=After

T=Threshold

A=Always and Never

P=Process

U=Under what conditions

L=Learn and Teach

T=Time-bound

Please understand there is no magic in the word "catapult." It is only a memory device. Let's take a look at each of the elements.

Change / Threshold Questions

Questions containing the words "change" and "threshold" are great ones to ask because they divide certain periods of time into specific windows that you can view. This makes your question relevant to the decisions being made now.

Both of these types of questions require specific answers from your prospect in terms of company leadership, circumstances, or numbers, all of which will give you tremendous leverage when making your proposal. You'll find that quite often prospects haven't thought in these terms, so they may have to work out an answer while they're talking. This can be a good thing, as it tends to lead to greater honesty and candor in their answers.

A "change" question gives you valuable comparative information about two separate periods of time. Things were going along, and then they changed. What caused the change? What happened because of it? Or what will happen if things change again?

Good to Great Questions: Change Questions

Good: Why are you doing this project?

Great: What has *changed* in the past six months that is motivating this project?

Good: What are you looking for in a new partner?

Great: What will have to *change* as a result of working with a new partner in order for you to declare the selection a success?

Good: How has the economic downturn affected you?

Great: What things have you *changed* over the past year that are giving you a margin of advantage in the market?

Good: What speed bumps do you think we might face during implementation?

Great: Historically, how has your organization resisted *change* when it comes to new business partners?

Good: How are things going with your new market implementation of [insert whatever business initiative your prospect has implemented]?

Great: What has *changed* in your marketplace since this decision that would cause you to come to a different conclusion now?

A "threshold" question gives you access to certain levels within one window of time. These questions work especially well when you're talking about performance and want to know: What performance threshold must be met in order for us to be successful? The answers can bring you really close to glimpsing the moment in which a potential vendor becomes a hired vendor.

Good to Great Questions: Threshold Questions

Good: How will you know if this project is a financial success?

Great: What performance *threshold* is necessary for you to reach in order to justify the costs of bringing on a new provider?

Good: Are you having any problems with your current supply chain delivery system?

Great: How do you measure your current *threshold* of satisfaction across your supply chain at each step?

Good: What kind of financial return are you expecting?

Great: Is there a *threshold* of ROI that has to be attained in justifying any project in your company, and if so, what is it?

Good: Are you expecting more from your vendors than you used to?

Great: In the last year, how has the performance *threshold* changed for the vendors you work with?

Always / Never and Learn / Teach Questions

These categories of questions help you set boundaries and working parameters that you will need to learn in order to work successfully with your prospect. Knowing the answers to these questions is important for a number of reasons. First, you'll find out if you should disqualify this prospect because you won't be able to work within the defined parameters. Second, you'll discover if this prospect has certain rules and regulations that must be followed without exception or if there is more flexibility. Third, you'll learn if the prospect is able to identify and learn from mistakes. And finally, you'll know how deeply committed the prospect is to certain issues, and how deeply rooted in the company those commitments are.

"Always" and "never" questions reveal baseline expectations. Answers to questions using "always" tell you what needs to happen every single time. For example, you might learn that contracts always have to be signed by a certain person. When you use "never" in your question, you want to know what will block you out and guarantee you'll lose if you engage in that behavior. For example, you might learn that the prospect never hires companies that aren't on a certain list, or wants all vendors to have corporate offices within thirty miles.

Good to Great Questions: Always / Never Questions

Good: What do you look for in a new vendor?

Great: Based upon your past experiences, what do you *always* insist upon with a new vendor?

Good: How have your criteria for vendor selection changed recently?

Great: As a result of the last selection process, what do you *always* insist upon in the answers you receive from vendors?

Good: What do you expect in terms of ROI?

Great: Is there a threshold of ROI that *always* has to be attained in justifying any project in your company, and if so, what is it?

Good: What don't you like about your buying process?

Great: If you could change your buying process, what one thing would you *always* do?

Good: What do you look for in a new vendor?

Great: What will you *never* tolerate with a new vendor?

Good: What kinds of things do new suppliers do that trip them up?

Great: When you are adding a new supplier, what are the things they *never* get right in the first month?

When you combine the "learn" and "teach" questions, you're trying to find out how deep into the organization the learning goes. Most often, when you ask what a prospect learned from an event or circumstance, you're asking what was significant enough that the company changed its behavior as a result. If the learning didn't cause a change in behavior, that's a sign the prospect didn't really learn much or that changing behaviors is not common inside this company.

Good to Great Questions: Learn / Teach Questions

Good: Are you ready to make a change in suppliers if you find at the end of our discussions that we can do a better job for you?

Great: In the last several years, when you have made a significant change in suppliers, what did you *learn* that you are *teaching* to all of your people?

Good: How has the recent downturn affected your company in terms of its hiring?

Great: What did your company *learn* during this economic downturn as it relates to this decision that you are *teaching* all of your people?

Good: What does it take to be a successful vendor with your company?

Great: What is the biggest lesson you'd like to *teach* prospective vendors so they could be successful in doing business with you?

Good: Do you make company-wide changes smoothly?

Great: Tell me about the last successful company-wide rollout of a new solution and what you think was *learned* from it.

Time-bound / After Questions

Business conditions are changing so fast that the circumstances under which your prospect was operating just a short twelve to eighteen months ago may not be the same now. When you ask general questions about how a company operates, you often get answers that are not grounded in recent events and therefore are not helpful.

By tying your questions to a specific time period (time-bound), you are able to focus the people to whom you are speaking on the most recent and relevant business environment. You also subtly create a sense that a change might be necessary because of the change in conditions. Finally, you are inviting a story—the kind of narrative that can give you greater information and context for the sales process.

Good to Great Questions: Time-bound Questions

Good: Why are you considering new partners now?

Great: *In the past six months,* what has changed that makes now the right time to consider a new partner?

Good: How have things changed lately?

Great: *Since the merger [or other triggering event],* what have been the biggest challenges in this area that you and your team have faced?

Good: Have you changed your requirements recently?

Great: *With the passing of the new regulation [or other triggering event],* what impact will this project have on your overall compliance requirements?

Good: Is your buying process always successful?

Great: *Within the past two years,* how would you score the vendors you have brought on using your buying process?

Good: Is there any change in your buying process?

Great: *Since the resignation of your CEO [or other triggering event]* was announced, how are buying decisions made?

An "after" question emphasizes a specific event and the effect it had on the company or the effect the prospect believes it will have in the future. These questions might be historical and give you information about the past (what did you do after that happened?). Or they might be hypothetical (what will happen after this event takes place?). In addition, "after" questions give you the opportunity to ask the prospect or client to project themselves into the future. This means that instead of asking a question that results in an answer of "We'll see how things go," you can anchor their responses to a specific triggering event.

Good to Great Questions: After Questions

Good: What's your vision for your company?

Great: In their ideal state, what will things look like *after* the transition to a new provider like us?

Good: What would "winning" look like if we work together?

Great: *After* what period will you know you have made the right choice?

Good: How would your employees respond to this project?

Great: What will be the internal response *after* you announce you are going to make this change?

Good: What are your feelings about the future of this project?

Great: What ROI must you see *after* implementations of this project is complete to make it successful for you?

Process / Under What Conditions Questions

If you're looking to land big deals, you need a solid understanding of the field you're playing on. **By asking a specific set of "process" questions early in your talks with prospective buyers, you can discover exactly what lies in front of you**—and whether or not you really want to pursue this potential deal.

Here's what you need to know about the buying process at each step that will help you move along more quickly:

- **People:** Who will be in the meeting at this stage of the project?
- **Decision maker:** Who is the decision maker for this step?
- **Decision criteria:** When companies don't move from one step to another, what are a couple of the reasons why they stall out at this point?
- **Time:** How long does each step take?
- **Next steps:** What is the next step after this one?

Good to Great Questions: Process Questions

Good: How many meetings do you think we'll have before you make a buying decision?

Great: What is the *next step in this process* and how long does it usually take to move through this current one?

Good: How do you know if your vendors are effective?

Great: How does your company analyze the effectiveness of its vendor selection *process*?

Good: Do you always follow your written sales process?

Great: Does your company ever alter the buying *process* in order to take advantage of an unusual opportunity?

Great: Under what conditions would your company alter its buying *process* in order to take advantage of an unusual opportunity?

Good: How long will it be before a buying decision is made?

Great: Within the past year, has your buying *process* gotten shorter or longer? Why?

Asking "under what conditions" questions are very valuable when you've hit some resistance in your process. If prospects are willing to think of conditions that will make it possible for you to work with them, then they are very interested in your proposal. No budget process is set in concrete. Finding out under what conditions a payment schedule would work can help you find ways to adjust your payment schedule and get several steps closer to final terms. If you can determine what ideal conditions would allow your prospect to move forward, you've won a major point toward landing the deal.

Good to Great Questions: Under What Conditions Questions

Good: Are you ready to make a change in suppliers if you find at the end of our discussion that we can do a better job for you?

Great: *Under what conditions* would you be willing to make a 100 percent change in providers?

Good: What is keeping us from moving forward with this project?

Great: *Under what conditions* will you be able to declare this project/program a success?

Good: Is there anything we should be sure to avoid?

Great: *Under what conditions* do companies trying to do business with your company usually trip themselves up?

Good: Are you able to make your purchase larger?

Great: *Under what internal conditions* would you consider doubling the volume of your purchase?

Never Ask a Prospect "Why"

Think of the last time you were asked, "Why did you do that?" Your immediate reaction is defensive, and answering puts you into a semi-hostile relationship with the questioner. Perhaps he or she was only asking for information, but the implication of wrongheadedness is there, and you feel it. The same will be true with your prospect. So often, through no fault of the person asking the "Why" question, it sounds challenging and attacking—even indicting.

There are three things you're actually trying to do when asking "why?" We'll examine them below, along with some alternative, more precise questions that will keep the other person engaged and relaxed while actually eliciting the information you're looking for.

1. Determine intentions

- "When you made the decision to go this route, what were the top one or two factors that brought you to this conclusion?"
- "Weighing all of the information, it sounds like you had to make a difficult choice. What made the difference in choosing this solution?"
- "In making this decision, there may have been a longer-term vision you were using in your selection. What were you aiming for in the long term?"

All of these questions help your prospect or client to feel validated that he or she made an intelligent decision at the time, even though in hindsight it may be apparent that it was the wrong choice. It is also possible that a poor choice was made, but with good intentions.

2. Determine choices

- "What would you have considered to be the riskier options at the time you selected this vendor?"
- "You may have been considering other options when you made this choice. What was the second-best option in your mind at that time?"
- "In making this decision, were there short-range, mid-range, and long-range alternatives? If so, into which category would you put this decision?"

These questions give context to the prior choice or decision, which is important in understanding how your prospect makes decisions—then and now. They also allow for narrative responses that will provide you with more information and create an expansive dialogue.

3. Determine circumstances

- "What were the business initiatives driving this choice at the time it was made?"
- "What has changed in your marketplace since this decision that would cause you to come to a different conclusion now?"
- "What do you know now that you didn't know when you made your choice that would cause you to make a different choice?"

These questions assume the truth of the old saying, "If I had known better, I would have done better." In creating that frame for the question, the prospect or client can admit that new decisions need to be considered based upon new circumstances.

Prospects may not answer "Why" questions because of embarrassment, ignorance, or arrogance. Whatever the reason, it's still our job to get to the underlying information and use it in the sales process.

If you ask the same questions as everyone else, you gain the same information as everyone else and gain no advantage in the process. You need unique information and unique insights. Of course, in order to be relevant and current with your prospect, you will also do the basics. This means going online and reviewing their websites and the commentary of analysts and bloggers, as well as taking a thorough look at all of the social media platforms where this prospect has a presence. While having these basics gives you no advantage, not having them will put you at a disadvantage compared to your competitors by conveying to your prospect that you didn't do your homework. This information can also point you in the right direction when formulating your CATAPULT questions and seeking the information that will give you an advantage in the sales process.

Chapter 15: Managing the Process

One of the core benefits of a structured selling process is that it helps you understand false positives and false negatives, as well as sort out when you are stuck. If sales were all about magic and relationships, then you would always be able to fall back on the simple idea that the deal didn't happen or the account went south because chemistry was wrong or the timing was wrong or the politics were wrong or the pricing was wrong. But these explanations really don't lend themselves to a continuous process improvement approach to improve your odds of winning next time. In contrast, when you have a well-articulated and defined selling process measured against a variety of accounts over time, you are able to start to identify patterns that let you improve your overall effectiveness in specific areas that need enhancement.

In Chapter 8, we talked about using the stage-gate process, as it's often called in manufacturing and construction, to set up standards and measures of progress. It's a process of project management that requires that certain things be accomplished at one stage before that stage is completed and a metaphorical gate opens, allowing you to go to the next stage. The stage-gate process explains why the second floor of a building is not framed before the basement has been dug and cemented in. As we've discussed, the stage-gate process can also be applied to the process of selling.

You know that an opportunity in your sales process is "stuck" when it stays longer in a stage than what you anticipate it should. Now remember, the reason an opportunity is stuck in a stage is because all of the things that are necessary for that stage to be completed have not yet been completed. We define these as the engagement gauges of people and information. If the right people from both sides of the buying and selling organization have not yet met and the right information has not been exchanged or revealed, then the gate cannot be opened to move to the next stage and sales process.

When you articulate a sales process in this structured way, quality replaces quantity as a measure of deal success. You increase the likelihood that you will win the deal. And you increase the chances of the deal being successful in the long run, because it has been properly and thoroughly conceived. Skipping stages, or jumping from an initial meeting to a proposal, is no longer valued. Compare this with the old school world of selling, where the number of proposals submitted was often used to measure the performance of sales representatives.

Over time, the stage-gate process also allows you to spot patterns where your sales effectiveness tends to slow down. When we slow down, that doesn't mean that we give up. It means that we need to implement a new strategy, technique, or approach in order to move the opportunity forward.

On some occasions, we may decide to abandon an opportunity because we believe that the reasons we are getting blocked cannot be overcome. In fact, one of the most important responsibilities of sales management and sales leadership in your organization is to tell you, as a sales representative, when to give up.

Now, I know that we cherish the idea of the ever-persistent salesperson, but in the large account sales world, the organization is making a great investment in supporting your efforts. Therefore, sales management and your organizational leadership have the right and the responsibility to tell you when your time would be better invested in other opportunities. Let's talk about why deals get stuck and what we can do about it.

Why Deals Get Stuck

There are four categories of reasons why a deal can get stuck:

1. Acts of God
2. Lies/Dreams/Governance
3. Wrong Problem
4. Wrong Chemistry

Each category has its own unique nuances, so your response to each will also be unique. But first, like a physician, before you can treat a problem, you have to diagnose. Step one entails determining what category of problem you have. Let's look at each in detail.

1. Acts of God

Acts of God are events over which you have limited or no control and that have such an impact on the sales process to the point that "stuck" may mean "dead." These include events such as weather, fire, the acquisition of your prospect's company, legal action, regulatory action, and reorganization. If a company is acquired or reorganized, you have very limited ability to change the priorities of the organization to focus on you. If a company's main manufacturing plant is destroyed by a tornado, the likelihood that they would want to meet with you anytime soon to discuss your new equipment sale is probably pretty low. If a company is under regulatory investigation, its senior management may not have the time and resources to speak with you, and your organization may not want to be tainted by the regulatory issue until it is resolved.

Strategy for Acts of God: Acts of God require that you step back and focus on other opportunities and let these rest. Of course, you'll check in to see if the issue has been resolved and if the opportunity door has swung open, but more than likely, you will not be able to influence or control the sales process until the big issue has been resolved.

2. Lies/Dreams/Governance

There are lots of reasons why companies participate in sales processes with outside organizations that do not include the idea of actually making a change. The four scenarios below happen on a regular basis. You have little to no control over the outcome, but they can suck up an inordinate amount of time and resources. Your job is to find out if any of these four are in play and then work with your sales leader to determine a plan of action, be it staying the course, changing the course, or leaving the field of battle.

Scenario 1: Dreamers, schemers, and fools. In many companies, there are people who fancy themselves to be the idea generators. They go out in the marketplace and look for solutions to problems that are priorities to them, but maybe not priorities to anyone else. These are the dreamers, schemers and fools. They don't have enough power to move a decision along, but they begin an investigative process to find potential providers of solutions to their pet problem and then suggest your solution or a solution like yours to higher-ups in the organization in order to win political favor and possibly a better work environment.

When you find dreamers, schemers and fools, realize that you are in a position of giving an enormous amount of information in the hope that this person will then influence someone else. These people do not often have the authority or influence that they claim to have and are wasting your time.

Strategy for Scenario 1: Identifying these individuals sooner rather than later is one more reason for taking steps early on to secure an Executive Sponsor—someone with the proper perspective to understand the buyer organization's needs and the authority to green-light the deal or advocate it to those who can.

Scenario 2: Letting you do their homework. Sometimes companies use a buying process to establish budgetary parameters or to obtain a market scan of solutions rather than do the work themselves. There was a time when organizations kept current with what was going on in the marketplace by attending trade shows or by securing some MBA class at a local university to do a market scan. Now, instead of doing their own homework, they send detailed RFPs, RFIs, or RFQs to the top providers in the marketplace. The resulting information they receive provides them with an in-depth and specific brief of what is available without their having to actually spend any time or money on their own behalf.

Strategy for Scenario 2: The best indicators of whether this is a homework assignment or a real opportunity are the ability of your contacts to define budget, time frame and what the threshold of performance for the outcome needs to be. If these cannot be expressed in real numbers it is a red flag. A red flag with a flare gun explosion is when you get the response, "Well, we're looking for you to tell us." These are not buyers, they are clowns without the floppy shoes and big red nose.

Scenario 3: Governance issues. We all know that companies typically require three bids when conducting an annual or cyclical review of vendors of particular products and services. They do this in order to make certain that they are still price-relevant in the marketplace, as well as to ensure that they have negotiating leverage in the upcoming contract review. Typically, there really isn't a sincere desire to move away from the current provider or incur the costs of making a switch, but they're able to kill two birds with one stone, gathering all the necessary information for negotiation and applying pressure to keep the current provider on his or her toes, while also meeting the compliance requirements of purchasing and procurement departments to ensure that there's an arm's-length transaction and adequate consideration in the marketplace of all options.

Strategy for Scenario 3: To determine whether this is governance driven rather than change driven, ask these questions:

- When was the last time that you changed your supplier and why? If the cycle is more than two bid cycles, it is likely not moving out. Remember, 88 percent of all opportunities go back to the incumbent.

- Why are you moving the business at this time? If the answer is unspecific, or reflects a desire to see what the market is offering at this time, it is unlikely they are changing.

- How have your needs changed in the last year that has changed the specifications for selection? If the needs have not changed, then the supplier more than likely will not.

Scenario 4: Inability to say "No." Believe it or not, this often happens. The nice guy syndrome thrives inside many companies. Because of the emphasis in many companies on reaching consensus, a culture of niceness is fostered that makes the idea of confrontation or of saying "no" to anyone, even someone outside of the company, distasteful to many people in the buying organization. Instead, they say, "Yes, later" or, "Let's come back to this in another quarter," or, "You'll be on our list for another review." These are all versions of "no," but they give false positives to hardworking salespeople such as yourself and siphon resources from your organization as everyone continues to believe that this is an active prospect.

Strategy for Scenario 4: Set expirations on all information requests to support your proposals, data requests and meeting requests. This means that when you ask for any of these three things, you let the buyer know that you need to get what you are looking for within a specific period of time or you will be unable to continue to participate in the process.

3. Wrong problem.

Often when a deal gets stuck, it's because we have defined the problem incorrectly for securing the involvement of the right types and level of people to produce a rigorous buying and selling process. There are a number of key reasons why this happens:

a) It's not a big enough problem. If the problem is considered too small to significantly move the performance metric needles of certain key decision makers, then it always falls on the "B-list" for that particular person or persons.

b) It's too big a problem. Often, organizations prioritize their problems by asking, "What resources do I have available to handle this problem?" If the problem is too big, the organization will decide to limp along with what's currently in place until the mythical time when there are resources sufficient to tackle the problem.

c) Your Executive Sponsor decides, "This is not 'my' problem." Your Executive Sponsor may decide that the problem as currently defined is really the priority of another department, person, or division. If your Executive Sponsor does not see it as "my" problem, then he or she will deflect, defer or delegate.

d) It's "not my boss's problem." Executive Sponsors often are operating underneath strong controls provided by their bosses in terms of setting priorities. They may see a problem as being significant to the organization and one that needs immediate resolution, but if their boss tells them that this is not the number-one priority, then they will step away from this problem and may seek to solve it later.

e) **It's a "not now" problem.** Timing is a critical driver in organizations when it comes to committing the resources to change. If there is the opportunity to delay, organizations will almost by default delay in switching from whatever they're doing now to something else. If you cannot create urgency around the resolution of a problem, the organization will delay.

f) **No one else thinks it's a problem.** A deal can get stuck if an Executive Sponsor sees the importance of a particular issue or problem, but no one else does, with the result that the Executive Sponsor can't secure any support from the buyer's table.

g) **Your Executive Sponsor will look bad if the problem gets solved.** As odd as it seems, sometimes Executive Sponsors see the resolution of a problem as actually making them look bad because the problem has been present for so long that they wind up having to bury it or expose the fact that they allowed it to last this long. As long as the problem looks unresolvable, then the Executive Sponsor looks like someone who is doing the best that he or she can, under circumstances for which there is no solution. This issue can arise if you propose a solution that could have been implemented at some earlier time. You'll find that the deal will become stuck as it becomes apparent to the Executive Sponsor that he or she will look worse by changing the situation than if the problem had just been left as it was.

Strategy for Wrong Problem: If you've identified that you have one of the seven criteria of having wrongly defined the problem, there are five things that you can do to improve your situation.

a) Add people to the buyer's table. If the problem is viewed as too big, too small, or not relevant for those at the table, the deal will stay stuck. By adding people to the buyer's table, you may be able to create a greater sense of appropriate scale and definition of the problem so that enough people see it as being relevant to them, of value to them, and of the right scale and level of necessity that they'll want to participate in the process, and the deal will get unstuck.

b) Reframe the Problem. If you reframe the problem according to your Executive Sponsor's parameters and you are now stuck, then it may be that only the Executive Sponsor sees the problem as being relevant and valuable. By increasing the size of the buyer's table, you can broaden and reframe the problem.

In a recent sales situation, the buying organization had posed the problem as a manufacturing problem. In discussions, the deal became stuck because the question became, "Who is the better manufacturer?" Manufacturing was viewed as a minimum standard of requirement that only a few met. Even though our company team met the requirement, our sales team reframed the problem from being one of manufacturing to being one of distribution. Once the frame was shifted from who was the better manufacturer to who was the better distribution provider, the sales organization could clearly demonstrate that it was the better distribution provider, and the deal became unstuck and moved forward.

c) Change the timeline. Organizations will start to slow down their purchasing process if they believe that they have a larger window of time in which to come to a conclusion. If you are not able to change the timeline, then your approach must be to change the perceived timeline and increase urgency so that the organization moves forward at a faster clip.

By creating an inflection point in which there is an understanding that if the decision is made now, better benefits can be gained, you can unstick that stuck deal. A better approach would be to show what the downside is of not taking action now. We know that penalty is more motivating than benefit to larger organizations when they're making decisions. By creating that inflection point, you can accelerate the process of making a decision.

d) Secure an additional champion. A stuck deal is evidence that your Executive Sponsor has a finite amount of influence over moving this process forward. Sometimes, you need an additional champion to come into the conversation to add the necessary political muscle and motivation to move the organization along.

e) Walk. Sometimes, you are unable to reshape the buying organization's perception of the problem. If this is the case, you need to stop expending resources on this organization and put the selling process on hold. It's possible to come back in two, three, four, or five months and revisit the discussion and see if the shape of the problem has changed, if the decision makers have changed, or if the urgency has changed. If one of those three elements has changed, the window of opportunity may reopen and you can revisit with more energy to see if you can land a deal. Always leave yourself the alternative of walking away from a deal that's not going to land.

4. Bad Chemistry

Often, there's bad chemistry between either the buyer's table members or a misalignment between the organization and your approach to the problem. There are four key ways to look at bad chemistry:

a) There's a switching cost issue. All organizations know that when they change from one solution to another or one product to another, there is a discrete or explicit switching cost. It's important that your representation of value fall within a range high enough to overcome the switching costs, yet at a level that is credible offering to the buyer; otherwise the buyer can become suspicious that you are claiming beyond what you can actually provide or that you will in some way make the people who are making the decision look bad.

b) Your solution is not a direct fit. When you provide a solution that has case studies that are not perceived as being dead-on perfect matches to what is being offered, there is a sense that what you are providing as justification for the decision is, in fact, not really valid. If you're not able to show that your solution is a direct fit, you'll suffer from a bad chemistry issue.

c) Personalities don't match. Sometimes people just don't get along. This is not unusual, in companies and out. However, when there's bad chemistry between individual players, individual departments, or in areas of the business, you will not win the business even if your solution is perfect, your cost justification is exactly right, and your understanding of the overall problem to be solved is accurate. Personalities do matter. I often say that sales is always about relationships, it's just not always about relationships. I would submit that as we move forward in this new world, trust is more important than what we call chemistry in relationships. When there is a personality mismatch, there is usually, inherit in that mismatch, a mismatch of trust.

d) Your answer lacks precision. There's a bad chemistry response if what you provide is nothing but platitudes and generalities. Organizations move forward because they have a high trust in what they're getting from you, and as part of that trust, they're looking for justifications that have statistical relevance. Soft benefits lead to slow sales decisions. If you can't provide some empirical, relevant measure by which the implementation of your product, service, or solution will make a measurable difference to that organization, the deal will slow down and get stuck.

Strategies for Bad Chemistry

There are four recommended solutions for dealing with bad chemistry.

a) Recalibrate the performance expectations. Sometimes, organizations have set their performance expectations in such a way that they are focused on the wrong things, perhaps looking at their switching costs or at their cost justifications. Try looking at what you are doing for the organization and gathering information from the people inside the buying organization so you can reset the outcome expectations for this particular solution. Helping the organization to justify its participation in the process may very well unstick the process.

b) Resubmit a more complete business case. When we hear from buying organizations that they are "still considering," I scratch my head and wonder, "What are they considering?" What they're considering is whether or not the business case is strong enough to justify the expenditure. If you're being told that they're still considering after an extended time, it's likely that your business case was not compelling enough. Companies may need a greater amount of detail in order to get one of the eels off the fence. Resubmit the business case with greater detail and accuracy. More statistical and empirical validation may help a stuck deal to get unstuck..

c) Add performance details and transition milestones to your plan. It can be hard to get organizations to take the first step because they don't see a way out. They see themselves as standing on one side of a chasm that they're going to have to cross in a single jump. More than likely, you have a transition plan from what they're doing now to what they'll be doing in the future. By fleshing out your transition schedule with performance details that they can understand as milestones that need to be achieved before moving forward to the next stage, you'll help them feel a greater level of control over the implementation process. This gives them comfort that if milestones are not being achieved, they can either back off or slow down implementation so that they're not taking as great a risk.

d) Change out the people. Sometimes the personalities in the room are just like oil and water. If so, there's no sense in trying to force these people to get along. Sometimes it's better for you to change out some folks to see if you can revive trust with one or more of the key decision makers.

Internal Reasons for Why Deals Get Stuck

For sales professionals, sometimes the greatest frustration is not about the prospect's getting stuck, but rather dealing with hindrances inside their own organization. If that happens to you, you must diagnose the problems before you can solve them. Here are three to consider.

1. False Affirmations. Often, we become pathologically optimistic about our own deals. Salespeople and executives alike may get involved with a deal that they really want and then can't see what's really happening at the table. They believe the reassurances they're hearing from the buying organization rather than looking at behavior and seeing cause for alarm. Repeated delays, the inaccessibility of key individuals, the unavailability of information are all excused and rationalized. There is a stubborn unwillingness to look at the stuckness for what it is.

It's the responsibility of every organization to look at the process as objectively as possible and, when there is data, respond to the data as data, not as something to be persuaded to ignore. If things are delayed, there's a reason, and that reason needs to be given full consideration. Remember the adage: "Trouble comes not on the hooves of elephants but on the flutterings of doves." When you see those flutterings, you must pay attention..

2. Internal resistance to calling out a stuck or dead deal. Sometimes, people don't like bad news. The CEO or the owner or one of the other senior executives in the organization doesn't want to hear that their pet deal is dying. So, instead of calling a spade a spade and putting an end date on the tombstone of the deal that has died, we keep it limping along in the pipeline, pretending that we don't know that it's dead.

Once again, pathological optimism creates a false expectation in the organization that revenue on this dead deal may miraculously occur. Sometimes it is better to face the ugly news than to carry forward an inconvenient truth.

3. False alarms. We all know the story of Chicken Little. People can panic when they see deals that are starting to slow down, especially those that the organization has invested a lot in and has high hopes for. While you don't want to succumb to pathological optimism, you don't want to be pathologically panicked when the deal hits speed bumps. Trust the process. Look for the data, follow your sales process, and understand that you can unstick a stuck deal by applying the strategies of the kind we're discussing in this chapter, rather than just throwing everything, including the kitchen sink, at the problem.

Overreacting to a deal that is starting to slow down also instills fear in the buying organization. Your panic sows doubt in the buying organization as to whether or not you are a safe partner in this venture.

One of the biggest challenges of the stuck deal is not to lose your head. When you lose your head, you lose their confidence. Better to react appropriately, follow a strategy, and move forward deliberately than to shout that the sky is falling.

Stuck deals are often why it's called "selling" rather than "order taking." If you want the glory, you've got to have guts. By deliberately navigating through the issues of a stuck deal and trying various responsive strategies, you will accrue the experience and develop the wisdom to know when it is time to walk versus when it is time to change your approach.

Chapter 16: Facilitating Trust and Solutions

I'm always surprised at the number of salespeople whose approach to preparing a sales presentation is about assembling a slide deck and pulling together some samples, a couple of case studies, and maybe a software demo. That's it.

That doesn't cut it anymore.

It may have worked in the past when customers were more patient and had time to allow for a long conversation that could meander through a variety of ideas, thoughts, and questions. No longer. People are looking for an efficient use of their time and expect you, as the salesperson, to drive the meeting.

The new world of preparation for any sales connection—be it a conference call, webinar, face-to-face meeting, site visit, audit, assessment, or whatever—is to have a fully developed and orchestrated front stage and backstage listing of all the events of that meeting. The best sales organizations leave nothing to chance and have a detailed preparation process to plan exactly how they are going to handle these interactions.

Where to start in this robust approach to preparing for a significant sales meeting (and from here on, when I use that word, I'm referring to any type of interaction between your company and the buying company)? I like to start with the people who will be in attendance from the buying organization. List the names. Now, for each name, make certain that you have identified answers to the following questions:

1. What does this person trust?
2. What does this person fear?
3. What does this person need to be persuaded of?

These three questions, in combination with an analysis of each person's position, title, responsibilities, and place at the buyer's table will give you an understanding of what you are truly trying to accomplish in the meeting.

When you understand all of this about your prospects who will be in attendance, several things become apparent.

First, you'll be able to determine who should be there from your organization. As you look at the buyer's side attendees, you'll see an appropriate matchup between each person's position and responsibilities with people on your team. There won't always be a direct overlap, but your goal is for each buyer's side attendee to hear your commentary as a selling organization through the voice of his or her equivalent or peer. Without this type of match-up, there is always the risk that there will be a mismatch in experience or a dissonance in relevant language that will, in one way or another, diminish the credibility of your company and your message.

Secondly, by understanding what the meeting attendees trust, fear, and need to be persuaded of, you are better able to choose the materials, arguments, and ideas that need to be presented. Too often, I see selling organizations prepare an agenda consisting of a list of topics to be covered during the presentation, coupled with a PowerPoint presentation that, predictably, addresses each point, with last slide inevitably reading: "Questions?". In my opinion, that is poor preparation. It is better to anticipate what each attendee fears, trusts, and needs to be persuaded of so that you can make certain that you only provide information that is relevant to each of the people in the room.

Research indicates that within twenty-four hours of a meeting, an attendee will only remember two to three core ideas and two to three core impressions. Within seventy-two hours, recollection drops to one core idea and one or two core impressions. The more directly you gear your presentation to your attendees' specific issues of trust, fear, and need for persuasion, the more likely it is that the ideas and impressions they remember will be those that can move the process toward a deal.

Thirdly, by selecting issues of concern to your attendees, you streamline your meeting agenda and increase the time that you're able to spend on those areas. Remember, you are not presenting to a company. You are presenting to individuals who have their own agendas and their own responsibilities set by others not in the room for relaying your information to their colleagues back at the office. The information they relay will be filtered through their perceptions. Did the information you provided confirm and affirm what they trust? Did it address what they were afraid of? As for whether it addressed what they needed to be persuaded of, the hope is that you will have done that by combining your past experiences with information from your Executive Sponsor and addressing what you believe to be the outstanding issues that need to be overcome in order for them to trust that your organization is the right choice.

Now let's talk about how you and your team should prepare to sell to this group. First, make a list of who from your organization should be there. Each person should be paired up with an attendee from the buyer's side.

Each person on your team is going to have no more than:

1. **Three tools:** These are diagrams, charts, samples, a plant tour, or any other physical prop for the presentation.

2. **Three points:** These are the key ideas to be conveyed regarding that person's area of expertise.

3. **Three questions:** These are core issues of information to understand the true pains and needs of the prospect as well as what approaches have failed in the past.

No more than three—and each of these is to be presented in the course of the meeting.

I have seen countless meetings in which people from the same company talked over each other, interrupted each other, contradicted each other, or looked at each other in quizzical silence, trying to determine who should answer a prospect's or customer's question. The result: diminished credibility of the presenting team. The role and content assignments I'm suggesting make each team member's responsibilities clear so the team can prepare and rehearse individually and together beforehand. That preparation results in an authoritative presentation that offers you greater control over the event and delivers greater substance and value to your prospect.

Be Unyielding in Your Preparation

Insist on giving all of the data to all members of your team as early as possible in the process. That includes a dossier on the target company, a profile of all participants in the buying process, and a copy of all communications regarding this deal.

Pick your team early. The team will shape the story, the key pitch points, the elements of "pitch theater," the chemistry, the manufacturing process—all of it.

Assign roles early. Your salespeople will do a better job of handling the job and of planning their time to do a good job. Don't get me wrong; this won't guarantee perfection. That's OK; the energy is potentially really healthy. My management tips are about containing and focusing that energy on what will help you to win.

Taking your team through various maneuvers ahead of the actual sales meeting will guarantee that everyone will know what to do. Preparation is priceless. Sometimes sales teams feel awkward about practicing in this manner. Don't worry about it. They'll begin to relax—and even enjoy—this prep work after a while. Once they get a taste of how effective such techniques are, they'll insist on doing them every time.

Make an Agenda

Your next step is to build an agenda. I touched on this elsewhere, but it bears repeating here: An agenda is not a list of talking points or subjects to be covered, or an itinerary of the discussion. **An agenda is a tool for controlling a meeting.** A good agenda has a strong influence on the final outcome of the meeting, and it exerts influence even before the meeting starts.

[Company] and Hunt Big Sales

Meeting [Date]

Agenda

Purpose: Generate a 30,000-foot view of a Strategic Account Acquisition Initiative with [Company].

Talking Points:

- Quick status update from [Company] on strategic account acquisition
- Quick status update from Hunt Big Sales
- What does success look like 1, 2, 3 years from now?
- What are the market and organizational challenges to a strategic account acquisition initiative?
- What resources and leadership resources are necessary for success?
- What case studies provide instructive models for the [Company] strategic account acquisition initiative?
- What is the map for developing a successful program?

Outcomes:

- Core Goals and expectations for a Strategic Account Acquisition at [Company]

We start constructing the agenda once we understand the attendees and their trust/fear/persuasion needs, and we start from the bottom of the agenda, first establishing the desired outcomes of the meeting, and work our way up. Take a look at the hypothetical sample agenda below for a meeting between our company, Hunt Big Sales, and another company.

When we constructed this agenda, the first thing we did was formulate the outcomes at the bottom. Outcomes of meetings should include the following:

1. A decision or choice
2. An assignment of resources and action items
3. A schedule or timeline for future events

Agendas such as this change the meeting, because you begin every meeting with the idea that at the end of this meeting, you will know something. You don't end with questions or next steps; rather, you will review the outcomes and say, "Have we achieved what we set out to achieve in this meeting as outlined by the agenda?"

Possible outcomes include a choice to do business or not do business, moving forward with resources to do an examination of needs, assignment of a team to work together to develop a proposal, or whatever you decide. But the mandate is that at the end of the meeting, you review that list of outcomes and determine whether or not you've accomplished them.

Once you've established the outcomes, then nail down the purpose of the meeting, which you put at the top of the agenda. The purpose of the meeting is all about the prospect or the customer. The language never focuses on you; rather, it focuses on, "Why are they coming to the meeting? What is the benefit to them? What will they get from this meeting?" The purpose should focus not outcomes, but on intentions.

Now, in between purpose and outcomes, there are the talking points of the meeting. These are generally three to five items that you are going to cover in the meeting as represented by the materials that you're going to provide and points your team will be making (as you've planned out above). These will reflect your plans for affirming trust and addressing fears and persuasion points that you've identified in those attending from the buying organization. The least important of all of the parts of the agenda are actually the talking points.

Prepare and "Peekaboo"

So, let's review. You have an assessment of the people who will be attending from the prospect company. You have an assessment of the people attending from your team. You know what needs to be communicated. You know what needs to be persuaded. Knowing all of this, you can now build your presentation materials.

Presentation materials should address only those items that will advance the process by addressing the concerns and questions of your prospect or customer. Eliminate everything that does not fulfill that requirement.

Now, you are going to "peekaboo" the agenda to your Executive Sponsor. See below. This peekaboo template gives you a rough script for introducing the agenda to your Executive Sponsor and asking for his or her impressions and feedback as to the likelihood of accomplishing this agenda with the attendees on the list (which has already been provided).

> (Executive Sponsor),
>
> Attached please find ______________ . As we discussed by phone, this is a confidential draft copy of ______________ for your review. If it is satisfactory, I will distribute the final copy to (name), (name), and (name).
>
> I will call you on (date), at (time) to discuss your thoughts so that I can incorporate them into the final document.
>
> Thank you for all of your assistance.
>
> Best regards,

Often your Executive Sponsor, after looking at the outcomes, will expand the number of attendees, because it becomes clear that you are approaching this meeting not from the point of view of: "What are we going to cover informationally?" but rather from the vantage of: "What are we trying to get done by the end of the meeting?" That's a good thing, and it should be encouraged. The great benefit of a peekaboo strategy is that it puts both you and your Executive Sponsor in agreement that during this meeting: we have a final outcome to accomplish.

Why is having an outcome so important? Because without it, meetings become mere information exchanges, and then at the end, the buyer organization usually says, "Well, we're going to have to go talk about this and get back to you." This leaves a fuzzy future for all involved. For you, things feel very unresolved, as you have no way to know whether you're going to actually move forward on this business or whether you're going to have to kill this opportunity because there really isn't a deal to be done.

Through the peekaboo, you've gotten a tacit contract with your Executive Sponsor that the people in the room are all going to be aimed at accomplishing the outcomes you've listed. If your Executive Sponsor wants to edit, add to, or even subtract from the outcomes of the meeting, you have the chance to discuss that in advance and see if together you can develop a better-quality meeting. That is good and productive collaboration. It also puts control of what will happen in the meeting in your hands and gives you an opportunity to have a preview of things that might happen in the meeting over which you would not have control. This is where having the Executive Sponsor becomes very, very valuable.

Warm the Room

Your next step is to warm the room. See below. I don't believe in going into rooms cold and presenting to people I'm meeting for the first time. The way to avoid that is to have your peer-to-peer contacts reach out by phone or e-mail in advance of the meeting and try to grab five minutes of phone time or an e-mail interaction with the person with whom they are going to meet. What you'll notice from the example addendum on warming the room is that each member who has a peer-to-peer connection in that meeting, conference call, or conversation reaches out in advance to offer an opportunity to interact.

Hello, **Mr. / Ms.**_______________ this is (**your name**) from (**your company's name**) and (**Executive Sponsor**) has told me that you will be joining us for our meeting on (**date/time**) at your offices. I'm looking forward to seeing you. I'm calling to briefly review our agenda and make certain I am prepared for any particular questions and ideas that you have.

The purpose of the meeting is (**purpose**). Our intended outcomes from the meeting are (**outcomes**).

If I can ask, what would make this meeting most valuable for you?

Is there any information you feel I should have before the meeting to make our time most productive?

If they don't get a chance to interact or connect by phone or e-mail, that's okay. What the reach-out accomplishes is that at the very beginning of the meeting, your peers can say to their peers, "We didn't connect by phone in advance. Sorry that we missed each other. Was there anything that you would like to add to today's meeting as far as outcomes?" Doing this puts in you in a position of controlling the discussion and the conversation and avoiding sidetracks and distractions.

Prepare Your Slides

Now it's time to build your slide materials, which should support the meaning you have built into all of the other pieces of the presentation. I have a preference for using no more than fifteen slides in a presentation session, if any slides are used at all. Why? Because slides are supposed to provide visual illustrations of compelling arguments. They are not supposed to be the compelling arguments themselves. You want everyone's eyes and minds on you, not on the screen.

Be Confident in the Knowledge That You've Done All You Can Do

Preparation like this is often deemed excessive by old-school sales representatives who like to show up and wing it. I think that is lazy and disrespectful to your prospect or customer and a disservice to your company that entrusts you with its message. Better to recognize that all of the people involved are busy professionals, and this is a serious business that requires the kind of preparation that leaves as little to chance as possible. When you prepare in the way that I've outlined in this chapter, you can feel good about how you met your professional responsibilities, no matter where the chips fall.

Final Thoughts

I want to tell you a personal secret. Landing big sales, amazing sales, is easy. It's not simple, but it is easy. There is a formula to it, and just like opening a safe, the right combination used in the right order will open the door to the vault.

Through my consulting work over the past ten years and in my twenty-five years of business experience prior to that, I have had the opportunity to work in almost every type of industry and marketplace for large sales. The core principles apply.

Of course, the transactional ways of doing business will continue for the peddlers and territory service teams. But in every place that they can be replaced by a more efficient way of conducting business, they will be. For us, the sales professionals, sales executives, and senior business leaders, the game has evolved to a new level. The greater our ability to effectively change to this new model, the more dramatically we will redefine the level of success that is possible in the realm of selling and business growth.

Works Cited

Cash, Jessica. Infographic: The Hidden Cost of a Failed Sales Manager. June 24, 2014. https://www.executiveboard.com/blogs/infographic-the-hidden-cost-of-a-failed-sales-manager/?business_line=sales-service.

CEB Global. *Sell How Your Customers Want to Buy*. 2015. http://www.executiveboard.com/exbd/sales-service/challenger/new-decision-timeline/index.page (accessed March 6, 2015).

Hubspot. *Marketing Statistics, Trends & Data - The Ultimate List of Marketing Statistics.* 2015. http://www.hubspot.com/marketing-statistics (accessed March 6, 2015).

Cash, Jessica. *Infographic: The Hidden Cost of a Failed Sales Manager.* June 24, 2014. https://www.executiveboard.com/blogs/infographic-the-hidden-cost-of-a-failed-sales-manager/?business_line=sales-service.

Johnson, Carla. 50 Statistics About B2B Sales And Marketing (Mis) Alignment. June 25, 2014. http://blogs.sap.com/innovation/sales-marketing/50-statistics-about-b2b-sales-and-marketing-misalignment-01253996.

Searcy, Tom. *Account Forensics - Sales Metrics You Should Be Focusing On.* October 31, 2013. http://www.inc.com/tom-searcy/sales-metrics-that-you-should-be-focusing-on.html (accessed March 6, 2015).

Oracle Marketing Cloud. *20 Stats Every Modern Marketer Should See.* 2015. https://blogs.oracle.com/marketingcloud/modern-marketing-stats (accessed March 6, 2015).

ChatterJee, Atri, and Andrew Gaffney. "B2B Buyer Behavior: Research into the New Preference and Expectations of B2B Buyers." DemandGen, 2012.

Acknowledgements

No one really reads the Acknowledgements section of a book except those people who are expecting to be acknowledged. Writing Acknowledgements is only part about gratitude - it is actually mostly about fear - the fear that you have left out someone who should be recognized.

There are so many people who deserve recognition that I am certain that I will have forgotten someone.

In no particular order...

My wife and family for their unwavering support in every aspect of my life including this and every book, workshop, or speech I create.

The clients of Hunt Big Sales - their energy and commitment to their companies inspires our team to do our very best to support them. Their experiences, and mine with them, form the core research of this book and its validation as "real" in today's marketplace.

Carajane Moore - a fantastic business partner, for all the sacrifices she makes for the business to run; and her support of all of the ideas we have - crazy or otherwise.

Toni Sciarra Poynter - the primary editor for this book and a true pleasure with whom to work (she says I don't have to do the "with whom" thing, but a little old school homage to writing is nice). Her work made this book so much better than it would have been.

Jessie Kelley - my Director of Production and my swearing, driving, detail partner in making this book happen.

Gretchen Foley and Ali Thomas for their help as research and production assistants as well as levity providers.

The faculty of Hunt Big Sales Academy - the sounding board, market laboratory assistants, and friends every writer should have to provide a true north.

Notes

Made in the USA
Columbia, SC
10 April 2021